The Urbana Free Library

9-02

WHY TEAMS CAN FAIL AND WHAT TO DO ABOUT IT:

Essential Tools for Anyone
Implementing Self-Directed
Work Teams

WHY TEAMS CAN FAIL AND WHAT TO DO ABOUT IT:

Essential Tools for Anyone Implementing Self-Directed Work Teams

Darcy Hitchcock

Marsha Willard, PhD

IRWIN
Irwin Professional Publishing
Chicago • Bogotá • Boston • Buenos Aires • Caracas
London • Madrid • Mexico City • Sydney • Toronto

Senior sponsoring editor:	Cynthia A. Zigmund
Project editor:	Denise Santor-Mitzit
Production supervisor:	Pat Frederickson/Jon Christopher
Designer:	Heidi J. Baughman
Compositor:	Electronic Publishing Services, Inc.
Typeface:	11/13 Times Roman
Printer:	Buxton•Skinner Printing Company

Library of Congress Cataloging-in-Publication Data

Hitchcock, Darcy E.
  Why teams fail and what you can do about it: essential tools for
anyone implementing self-directed work teams / Darcy Hitchcock.
Marsha Willard.
    p. cm.
  Includes bibliographical references and index.
  ISBN 0-7863-0423-5
  1. Self-directed work groups. I. Willard, Marsha L. II. Title.
HD66.H579 1995
658.4'02—dc20   95–805

Acknowledgments

The learnings and ideas shared in this book are the result of the collective wisdom of many clients and colleagues. We are grateful to all who spoke with us and who allowed us into their organizations to learn with them. We would especially like to thank those individuals who granted us interviews and were willing to share their stories—good and bad. These include:

Chris Avalos
Dennis Bowman
Eva Caradonna
Wallace Carey
Loren Cogdill
Jean Copley
Deb Daniels
Jeff Davis
Dave Eberhardt
Kimball Fisher
Bill Frohmayer
Jim Gladen
Lee Hebert
Morgan Horne
Roseanne Ierulli
David Kenney
Barb Kohler
Jeff McAuliff
Jerry Miller
Roy Montague
Linda Moran
Dave Phillips
Tony Reyneke
Kim Varney

Preface

People are always eager to talk about their successes, but most are more reticent when it comes to their mistakes and failures. Yet we all have at least as much to learn from mistakes as from successes. It is in this spirit that we write this book. We want to share the most common pitfalls organizations encounter when implementing self-directed teams and explain how to avoid them.

Self-directed work teams (SDWTs) are still largely in a honeymoon period. While they date back to the mid-1940s as a studied phenomenon, they are only recently being accepted as an appropriate strategy for improving organizational performance. Interest has been piqued by articles with such titles as "Who Needs a Boss?" (*Fortune*) and miracle stories such as those told about Federal Express, Xerox, and Chaparral Steel. Enthusiasm is growing as organizations in all industries explore self-direction. Today one in five organizations has implemented or is in the process of implementing self-directed work teams, up from 1 in 20 just a decade ago. Charles Manze, associate professor of management at Arizona State University, predicts that by the end of the century, 40 to 50 percent of all workers will be managing themselves in teams.[1]

With this growth in popularity will come failures, and with failures disenchantment. Kimball Fisher, a well-known consultant and author in the field, has let slip an ugly little secret:

> SDWT's don't always, of course, produce sterling results. Although I am not aware of any studies to confirm this, SDWT consultants normally suggest that teams have about a 50% success rate.[2]

---

[1] Joan Lublin, "Trying to Increase Worker Productivity, More Employers Alter Management Style," *The Wall Street Journal*, February 13, 1992, p. B1.

[2] Kimball Fisher, "Diagnostic Issues for Work Teams," in Ann Howard (ed.), *Diagnosis for Organizational Change* (New York: Guilford Publications, 1994), p. 258.

That figure might be great in baseball, but it's not great in business. Given the time, resources, and headaches associated with implementing such wholesale cultural change, we must find a way to improve the hit rate.

Certainly the choice is not to return to traditional management practices, for self-direction has withstood 50 years of research proving it is a better way to manage in most situations. Alternatively, creating a fail-safe implementation process is impossible. What we *can* do is share with you the mistakes we have seen organizations make so that you do not make the same ones.

We base this book on our years of experience as consultants helping organizations implement self-direction and also our experience in managing and working within teams. We supplement the content with research studies we have conducted. Since organizations are understandably reluctant to broadcast their mistakes, we have had to obscure many of their identities, but all the stories we tell are true.

WHO SHOULD READ THIS BOOK

Many types of teams exist. In this book, we focus specifically on the problems associated with self-directed teams, natural work groups that share most or all of the responsibilities of a traditional supervisor. They are also sometimes referred to as *self-managed*, *semiautonomous*, or *high-performance* teams.

This book can help anyone interested in or already implementing self-directed teams. Executives, managers, change agents, facilitators, and team members can all benefit from the insights.

If you are just learning about these teams, Part I will help you discover what self-direction is and what foundation is necessary to start. Chapter One contains a "Red Flag Assessment" that will help you decide whether self-direction is even appropriate in your situation.

Organizations just beginning the implementation can glean important insights about how to proceed, eliminating some of the frustrations and problems others have encountered.

For those who are in the midst of implementing SDWTs, early chapters may help you diagnose your existing challenges. Later chapters will help you foresee upcoming hurdles so you'll be able to run around them or leap them with room to spare.

Organizations which have stumbled and fallen along the path to self-direction can use this book to re-energize their effort, diagnose their mistakes, and begin anew.

HOW TO READ THIS BOOK

This book can be read from cover to cover, providing a thorough understanding of self-direction and the challenges it entails. Or you can pick and choose the chapters which seem to deal with the most pressing problems your organization is facing. It is not meant to replace the guidance of a knowledgeable consultant or be a step-by-step manual. Instead, consider it a guide book, something to suggest things to do and places to avoid on your journey. Hopefully you'll take it with you and refer to it often. The following chapter summaries may help you decide where to begin.

PART I: STUCK IN THE STARTING BLOCKS

The chapters in Part One address issues that prevent organizations from even beginning the journey toward self-direction:

Chapter One, "Why Bother?", explains what self-directed teams are and dispels some of the common myths about them. The chapter also discusses how to overcome complacency and explains why formulating a clear need to change is so important.

Chapter Two, "But It Sounds So Scary," addresses what people fear most about moving toward self-direction. Managers, technical specialists, unions, and employees all have reason to fear this change. We provide concrete actions and activities to help turn their fear into enthusiasm.

Once people grapple with their fears, their focus turns outward. Chapter Three, "'They' Aren't Ready," covers the beliefs about others that prevent people from beginning the journey. Managers often think employees aren't ready; employees usually think the opposite. Unions and management each tend to wait for the other party to make the first move. This chapter shows how to break the stalemate.

PART II: FALSE STARTS

Part II deals with problems organizations encounter early in the implementation.

Chapter Four, "Where Do We Start?", addresses how to implement self-directed teams. Before discussing common pitfalls, we provide a flexible yet structured process for implementing teams and explain the structures (such as steering committees) that are usually used.

Chapter Five, "Who Should Be on the Team?", helps to answer the question "How do we structure the teams?" This chapter focuses on the role and struggles of those who must decide how to translate the concept of self-direction into concrete actions.

Lack of clarity about what empowerment means is a common pitfall. Chapter Six, "Now We Can Do Whatever We Want, Right?", clarifies the new responsibilities teams assume in conjunction with their new rights. We provide a structured process for defining roles and responsibilities.

Chapter Seven, "We Put You in Teams, So Why Aren't You Working?", explains the support necessary for teams to succeed. In addition to explaining the roles of champion, consultant, and facilitator, we cover in detail the development needs of managers, since managers are critical to the success of these teams.

PART III: KNOCKING DOWN HURDLES

Part III addresses longer-term issues that can impede or reverse the progress of teams.

Chapter Eight, "Who Sets Goals and Measures?", explains how to design goal-setting and measurement systems to support teamwork instead of individual work. We include a worksheet to help you design a balanced set of measures.

Chapter Nine, "How Do We Appraise and Reward Performance?", explains why performance appraisal and compensation systems must be radically redesigned to support teams. We provide specific guidelines for reinventing these systems.

Chapter Ten, "Close Encounters with the Law," explores the legal issues associated with self-directed teams and provides practical guidance for avoiding legal missteps.

Organizations seem to work hard to avoid learning from their own successes. Chapter Eleven, "The Immune Response," explores the challenges associated with expanding self-direction into the rest of the organization.

Chapter Twelve, "Bait 'n Switch," addresses threats presented by events beyond the control of the organization like turnover of leadership and downturns in the economy. We provide tips for holding self-direction together during these turbulent times.

PART IV: BEYOND SELF-DIRECTION

Self-direction is just one stop along a fascinating journey. In Part IV, we look beyond what most organizations believe is possible. Chapter Thirteen, "Democracy in the Workplace: Can It Work?", shares several real-world examples of organizational democracy in which employees are involved in setting organizational strategy. While not every organization will choose to pursue this approach, we invite skeptics and missionaries alike to stretch their assumptions about what can be achieved.

Darcy Hitchcock
Marsha Willard

Contents

P A R T

I

STUCK IN THE
STARTING BLOCKS

F ar more organizations should be implementing self-directed work
  teams (SDWTs) than are currently doing so. Some have let their past
successes blind them to the demands of the future. Others shy away from
SDWTs despite their needs for quantum leaps in performance. Their
employees feel aimless and disenchanted, while their customers are frustrated or even hostile. The chapters in Part I explore why these organizations are stuck in the starting blocks.

Chapter One, "Why Bother?", explains why many organizations do not
even consider self-direction. They may hold misconceptions about self-
directed teams, such as that such teams work only in manufacturing or
that they represent anarchy. Others are complacent about their current situation, oblivious to the dramatic changes in our economy. Many have not
clearly tied their strategic needs to the benefits SDWTs can bring.

In Chapter One, we define what self-directed teams are and what they
are not. We address each of the barriers just mentioned. Take the Red
Flag Assessment on pages 7 and 8 to discover whether teams are appropriate for your organization. We also provide a step-by-step process to
help you make a case for change in your organization.

Once people understand what self-direction is and how it can benefit
the organization, they may still resist the change. They want to know

"What's in it for me?" Chapter Two, "But It Sounds So Scary," explores people's personal reasons for not wanting to pursue self-direction.

Every population has reason to fear the changes self-direction may bring. Managers fear loss of power and control. Technical specialists fear loss of status and their specialized knowledge. Unions fear that SDWTs will eliminate the need for them altogether. Employees usually fear that SDWTs are just management's way of getting them to do more work for the same pay. In Chapter Two, we take on each of these fears and provide specific suggestions for overcoming them.

Even after deciding that self-direction may bring personal benefits, people can still find an excuse not to move forward. They shift the focus from themselves to others. Chapter Three, "'They' Aren't Ready," discusses the beliefs about others that inhibit progress. Managers routinely underestimate the ability and readiness of their employees. Conversely, many employees are convinced that their managers aren't ready to share power. In union settings, management and union often glare across the negotiating table, each waiting for the other to make the first move.

We show you how to end these stalemates in Chapter Three. Recognize, however, that in the race to achieve self-direction, not everyone is equally prepared. Some stand at the head of the pack, ready to assume more responsibility, while others lag behind, questioning whether the race has any value at all. In this chapter, we describe the phases of personal empowerment that each person travels on the road to self-direction and discuss what needs to be done to help them progress to the next stage of their development.

After reading Part I, you should be able to decide whether self-direction is appropriate for your organization. If it is, you will know what must be done to lay a strong foundation for its implementation.

Chapter One

Why Bother?

W hile it may seem odd, one reason organizations fail with self-directed teams is that they never begin. In many organizations, implementing self-direction would be an appropriate performance-enhancing step, but leadership censors the idea. In this chapter, we will examine common reasons organizations fail to consider self-direction when it would be in their best interest to do so.

Often self-direction seems like such a radical departure from past practices that leaders don't see the need for such drastic changes. Leaders often are also confused about self-direction, thinking it means the absence of leadership. Also, many organizations have not made self-direction a top priority because they do not understand the link between their strategic needs and the benefits self-direction can offer.

In this chapter, we address three issues that prevent organizations from considering self-directed teams: misconceptions, complacency, and strategy. We clarify misconceptions about self-direction and provide a clear model to explain the beliefs on which it is based. We discuss how to reframe the situation so that executives can see why successful past practices may lead to future problems. We also provide a process for deciding whether self-direction should be a critical strategy in your organization.

MISCONCEPTIONS ABOUT SELF-DIRECTION

Many organizations hold serious misconceptions about self-direction that prevent them from exploring this option. Some know that self-directed teams exist in manufacturing settings but assume they won't work in their environment. Others equate self-direction with anarchy. Perhaps most damaging of all, some perceive the outward manifestations of these teams as the essence of self-direction.

Self-Direction and Anarchy

A number of myths exist about self-directed teams. Let's clear up some of the confusion.

Self-directed teams cannot do whatever they want. Period. Nor are they leaderless groups in which no one seems to know what's going on. What is a self-directed team? Here is our definition:

> A self-directed work team is a natural work group of interdependent employees who share most, if not all, the roles of a traditional supervisor.

Those words were chosen carefully, so let's emphasize a few important points.

First, a self-directed team is a natural work group, meaning that team members work together full time. It is not a warmed-over quality improvement team that meets only one hour a week. A true self-directed work team is defined by a clear and common purpose that establishes a sense of mutual accountability among team members.

Second, SDWTs include interdependent employees—those employees who must work together to complete a whole process, product, or project or to serve a set of customers. This often implies redrawing the organization chart. For example, maintenance technicians often report to maintenance. However, they are often less interdependent with one another than they are with the operators they serve. This is often the case with other support or staff groups as well. Self-direction may mean decentralizing certain tasks and reassigning people to the line teams.

Third, the employees share the responsibility of managing themselves. Some organizations create one leadership position on a team, commonly referred to as a *team leader*. If you give this person all the powers of a traditional supervisor, you will create a straw boss, not a self-directed team. That's cheating. It also fails to force all team members to take responsibility for themselves. The simplest way to avoid this problem is to break the job of a traditional supervisor into logical chunks and assign those chunks to different individuals (or groups of individuals) on the team.

Fourth, the team assumes most, if not all, the responsibilities of a traditional supervisor. That implies a spectrum of self-direction, from a little self-directed to a lot. Practically all self-directed teams assign their own work, assess their work, coordinate vacation schedules, solve technical problems, and lead team meetings. Many self-directed teams give feedback to peers, set annual goals, interview job candidates, and purchase materials. Fewer self-directed teams fire co-workers, decide how to handle layoffs, determine team compensation, or have input into long-term strategy.

It is important that self-direction be viewed not as a destination but as a process. The teams do not start out totally self-directed, nor do they ever totally get there. There is always something new for them to learn, a new responsibility for them to assume.

In addition to the main points emphasized above, there are other common, though less universal, attributes of self-directed teams. For example, many self-directed team members are cross-trained in one another's work so that they can rotate positions or fill in during vacations and bottlenecks. They are often composed of 4 to 12 employees, although smaller and larger teams exist. While social psychologists recommend an ideal team size of six to eight members, the actual size of the team should be determined by the work, not by some artificial standard.

Don't They Just Work in Manufacturing?

Self-directed teams as an identified and researched phenomenon date back to World War II. Many early examples of successful teams were in so-called blue-collar positions such as mining and manufacturing. Some people have taken this to mean that self-directed teams work only in manufacturing. This is patently not the case. Self-directed teams have been proven to work in a wide variety of cases, even in situations where common sense dictates they should not. Here are some interesting examples:

• *Union environment.* Steelmaker LTV Corporation uses teams in its galvanizing plant in Cleveland. The employees hire their co-workers. They have no job classifications; instead, people are paid based on skills they acquire. LTC's staffing levels are approximately one-half of what they would be at a conventional steel plant.[1]

• *Paperwork.* Consolidated Freightways, a trucking company that provides a self-insured medical plan for its nonunion employees, redesigned its paperwork process for handling claims so that teams would be assigned to specific divisions or subsidiaries of CF. The pilot team, after operating only a couple of months, reduced the processing time for medical claims from 5 weeks to approximately 10 days.

---

[1] John Holusha, "LTV's Weld of Worker and Manager," *The New York Times*, August 31, 1994, pp. C1–C4.

• *Health care.* Mercy Hospital has eliminated service delays, reduced the number of people with whom patients must interact, and improved patient care by creating empowered "care" teams. These teams are made up of four types of professionals: a clinical partner and a technical partner (licensed professionals such as nurses, dieticians, and therapists), a service partner (who manages housekeeping and supplies), and an administrative partner (who does admitting, medical records, and financial advising). Clinical decisions are made by councils made up of staff who work closely with patients.[2]

• *Food service.* Chick-Fil-A found a way to work around oppressive turnover (commonly 200 to 300 percent in the fast-food industry). Implementing teams in a turbulent work force might seem impossible, but Chick-Fil-A has made it work. It reduced labor costs, improved customer satisfaction ratings by as much as 20 percent, and improved profitability. It has also reduced turnover to approximately 110 percent, an added benefit.[3]

• *City government.* The New York City Sanitation Department, which collects the garbage of over 7 million people, was in shambles in 1978. Only one-half of its 6,500 trucks and sweepers were operational on any given day. Three years into its efforts to hand off decision making and day-to-day control to line workers, 85 percent of the fleet was back in service. This and other activities saved the city $16 million.[4]

• *Law enforcement.* Madison, Wisconsin, implemented an Experimental Police District composed of 38 employees and covering a jurisdiction of over 30,000 citizens. Employees elected their own captain, developed their own work schedules, and even designed and built their own district building. They further involved their constituents in a community-oriented policing system. A survey of employees showed that 80 percent were more satisfied with their jobs, while 60 percent believed they were better at solving crimes. Absenteeism and worker compensation claims dropped significantly as well.[5]

• *Downsizing.* Alliant Techsystems, a defense technology supplier located near Seattle, implemented self-directed teams while reducing its

2"Laying the Groundwork: Organizational Design," Episode 107, *Taking the Lead* (Pasadena, CA: A televised production of INTELECOM Intelligent Telecommunications, 1994).

3Mark Miller, presentation at the Clemsen University Benchmarking High-Performance Work Teams Conference, March 17, 1994.

4David Osborne and Ted Gaebler, *Reinventing Government* (Reading, MA: Addison-Wesley, 1992), pp. 259–61.

5Ibid.

work force by approximately two-thirds over a four-year period. The division was spun off from Honeywell in 1991, when the defense industry was just beginning to enter into a period of consolidation following the end of the Cold War. Major contracts were terminated and some new ones were lost after the spin-off. Despite the potentially demoralizing effects of these changes, Alliant's Marine Systems employees pulled together into cohesive teams. These changes enabled them to reduce their cycle time by 50 percent or more in some cases.

• *Temporary teams.* At Intel, where the rapid pace of change makes rigid job assignments impractical, most employees are assigned to one or more project teams. In this environment, a hierarchical structure is not only unfashionable but untenable as well. When pressed to identify a reporting structure, team members frequently respond, "We report to each other." Workers take their cues not from a supervisor but from the demands of the project.[6]

• *Competition from cheap overseas labor.* Teams have fared so well at Xerox since their introduction in 1982 that the corporation will bring 300 jobs back to New York from overseas. It expects to realize higher quality as well as a savings of over $2 million a year.[7]

The message in these diverse examples is that self-direction has worked successfully in almost all industries. It has also worked in diverse cultures—the United States, Brazil, India, and Sweden, to name a few. Self-directed teams honor certain basic principles about Homo sapiens. Most people like to work in small groups that are responsible for a whole piece of work, most like to use a variety of skills, and most like flexibility and control over how they do the work. While it may not seem so to those who have been indoctrinated into the industrial age workplaces of assembly lines and chains of command, self-directed teams are a more natural way to work.

Red Flag Assessment

Having made the case for the broad applicability of SDWTs, we should explain that there are certain conditions under which self-directed teams won't work. The critical characteristics relate not so much to the type of

---

[6]William Bridges, "The End of the Job," *Fortune*, September 19, 1994, pp. 62–74.

[7]Aaron Bernstein, "America Needs Unions, But Not the Kind It Has Now," *Business* Week, May 23, 1994, pp. 70–82.

work but to the workplace. Take this Red Flag Assessment. A *no* to any question should cause you to reconsider the efficacy of teams at this time.

1. Is top management/leadership committed to involving employees?
2. Will top management be around long enough to see the implementation through (two to five years)?
3. Are the employees interdependent? Do they need to work together to complete a process, product, or project or to provide a service?
4. Are self-directed teams a high enough priority that they will get the time and resources necessary to make them successful?
5. Does the work or work schedule allow employees time to think, meet, and discuss ideas?
6. Are the employees technically competent in their work?

Assessment Explanation

Question 1: Support at the top. While executives may not be able to foresee all the ramifications self-direction will have on their behavior and their organization, they must believe that involving employees in decision making and self-management will be good for the organization. *Top management* is a relative term, however. In a mega-corporation, a plant manager or division director is sufficient to get started. This individual should oversee a work group that is relatively autonomous and protected from other parts of the organization.

If you do not have a high-level champion but still want to proceed in the hope that his or her support will be forthcoming, here are some tips. First, take a low-key approach. Don't flaunt the words *self-directed teams* or *empowerment*. Instead, keep talking about "doing things differently to better serve the customer and improve performance." Quietly, over time, share more and more of your responsibilities with your employees.

Second, track your performance improvements. When others begin to notice you are doing things differently, you had best have compelling data showing bottom-line performance improvements.

Third, talk openly with your team about the inherent risks of proceeding without a champion, and devise methods for supporting one another when resisters throw up roadblocks.

Finally, establish an intimate network with others who are moving toward self-direction so that you can learn from them without incurring noticeable training costs.

Question 2: Changes in leadership. Implementing self-direction requires a long-term commitment. A change in leadership is one of the most common reasons for the implementation collapsing. While we share some strategies for mitigating a leadership change in Chapter Twelve, it might be best not to begin an organizational change of this magnitude until leadership has stabilized.

Question 3: Interdependence. While the degree of interdependence may vary, employees need a reason to work together if they are to be formed in teams. However, if your initial answer is that your work group is not interdependent, consider whether members are interdependent with others in the organization. In functional organizations where departments are formed around people of like skills, the employees are often more interdependent with other departments than with one another, and you should consider redrawing the organizational boundaries. This is often the case with support groups such as maintenance, engineering, purchasing, and so on.

Question 4: Priority. The self-directed team graveyard is littered with teams that did not receive adequate support and training. An initial one-day workshop does not begin to fulfill their needs. And management will find that implementing these teams may consume 30 to 50 percent of their time in the early stages. We tell managers, "You can have three priorities; I don't care what two of them are, but one has to be teams."

Question 5: Time. Knowledge work requires discretionary time. If your employees are chained to a machine for every moment of their workday, self-direction will not work. However, just because the employees appear overworked now is not necessarily a reason not to implement teams. Think of it as a tile game (the little plastic game that involves moving lettered tiles around to make words). You have to make the open space in the middle before you can move the tiles around. If your employees' tile game is full, you have to find a way to make the space. High-leverage strategies include re-engineering the process, changing technology, outsourcing part of the process, working overtime, or getting relief workers. Once your employees have time to begin making improvements, the space in the center will get bigger, more than paying back the initial investment that created the first gap in the board.

Question 6: Technical competence. You don't drop the reins unless you know the horse knows the way back to the barn, so you shouldn't empower employees who don't know what to do. Give these employees technical training before you give them responsibility to manage their own work.

Self-Direction as a Management Philosophy

As we have consulted with organizations over the years, our clients repeatedly have asked very specific questions in their quest for understanding: How many people must be on a self-directed team? Does a team have to do budgeting to be self-directed? Can our existing department be a self-directed team? To all these questions we would answer, "It depends," which did little to clarify the issue and a lot to frustrate our clients.

We finally realized that they didn't understand that self-direction is neither a structure, a set of responsibilities handed off, nor a group of a certain size. Self-direction at its core is a set of beliefs about how to run an organization. It is a management philosophy. Once clients understand the philosophy and the assumptions on which it is based, they can answer the specific questions for themselves. We will explore this philosophy in more depth in later chapters; here we will discuss the basic tenets.

Managers have two basic choices of management philosophy: They can be parents or they can be partners. Traditional management practices represent the former option. Based on scientific management practices formulated by Frederick Taylor around the turn of the century, managers were to think and employees were to work. The basic premise that managers should plan, organize, control, and direct and then tell employees what to do is predicated on a belief system that includes the following notions:

- Employees do not know what to do and so must be directed.
- Employees cannot be trusted to do the right thing on their own, so they must be supervised.
- Employees will look out only for their own self-interests and will do as little as possible. Thus, the organization needs to "motivate" employees through a variety of methods, including goal setting, performance appraisals, job standards, and rewards.
- Employees are motivated primarily by money; when money doesn't work, try fear.

Just as parents set the rules at home and have the sole power to punish, managers in traditional organizations are expected to establish policy and discipline employees. Just as parents are not expected to live up to the same standards as their children (e.g., be in bed by 9:00), managers receive more perks than employees do. Just as children are the property and responsibility of parents, so are employees to managers, disposable resources to be hired and fired at will.

As distasteful as this analogy may be, its parallels are too strong to ignore. Both are relationships based on dependency. However, the situation is not all bad. It can be comforting to work for managers who are responsible for taking care of you and who worry about the big picture for you. Many employees have become accustomed to the entitlements and freedom from responsibility that spring from this philosophy. Most parenting managers are not ogres, either; they simply do more for their employees than employees need as adults.

Self-direction is predicated on a different set of assumptions that must be held as self-evident:

- Employees want to do a good job.
- Employees possess relevant knowledge and are a resource.
- Employees should be trusted until proven untrustworthy. We can expect them to keep the interests of the organization at heart.
- Employees are motivated primarily by pride, achievement, accomplishment, and other intrinsic motivators. Recognition and a fair reward system are only supplements.

With these foundation beliefs, it is possible to forge a partnering relationship with employees in which managers need not be omniscient and employees have a right to be involved in decisions that affect them. It is fundamentally a different system that leads to different responsibilities and behaviors. We will explore these more fully in Chapter Six.

Using this understanding, let's return to answer the questions posed before.

How many people should be on a team? As many as needed to get the work done and meet the needs of the organization.

Does a team have to do budgeting to be self-directed? If it makes more sense for the manager to keep this responsibility, the answer is no. If the team is simply intimidated by the responsibility, the answer is yes; they should eventually do budgeting, because otherwise they will be asking their manager to be a better parent, not a partner.

Can our existing department be self-directed? Yes, if you are operating as partners. Self-direction is as much a management style as it is a way of structuring.

COMPLACENCY (WE'VE DONE IT THIS WAY FOR YEARS)

Many leaders are familiar with self-direction but do not see the need for it in their organization. Occasionally they are correct; usually they are complacent.

Complacency, the willingness to let things continue as they are, can stem from two sources: We mistake the cause of our success, or we fail to recognize that the rules have changed.

Confusing Cause with Correlation

Humans often confuse cause and correlation, attributing meanings to actions that have no effect on results. We spit on dice in the hope that they will come up sixes; we carry an umbrella in the hope that it won't rain; and we step on the gas before turning the key in our fuel-injected cars. Old habits die hard. We decide, often incorrectly, that our behaviors are primarily responsible for the results.

In the United States, many organizations believed for decades that we were somehow superior to all other nations. We were more productive; we had a positive balance of trade; everyone wanted to be like us. We attributed this success to how we ran our organizations. Our success, however, was more the result of not having most of our factories bombed in World War II. While Japan and Europe struggled to rebuild, the United States enjoyed an unprecedented period of growth.

Today, of course, many other nations have risen in prominence and are benefiting from their more modern facilities. This has caused upheaval in our manufacturing sector first, but there is reason to assume that the same upheaval will occur in other sectors as well.

Within organizations, leaders can make the same mistake: thinking that correlation implies a cause. Many managers believe their get-tough management style is responsible for the superior performance of their employees; instead, that performance may have resulted *despite* their management style.

In any case, leaders who misdiagnose the reasons for their success may be blind to the need to change. And self-direction threatens some of the most cherished premises of the old guard. Given their point of view, they would have to be insane to choose teams.

The New Economy

Even if you accurately determine the root cause of your past success, this does not ensure your success into the future. Many great organizations, including IBM, Kodak, and General Motors, have discovered that practices that had made them great were now killing them. We are entering a new economy, one driven by entirely different factors. As Joel Barker has noted, when the paradigms change, everyone goes back to zero; past success means nothing. Just as the Swiss watchmakers lost their grip on the market when quartz technology became the standard, similar transformations are possible in all sectors of our society.

The Industrial Revolution rode in on rails. Along with mass production, easy access to transportation, cheap labor, and raw materials were the key factors driving success. The competitive standard was productivity: Could you produce the largest number of goods or provide the largest volume of services at the lowest cost?

Since Ford's first assembly line, the world has changed. Markets are becoming specialized and fragmented. Many products rely on computer chips made from one of the most abundant materials on the planet, silicon. With a higher standard of living, people are willing to pay for quality. Now the primary resource of any organization is not raw materials or cheap labor but information. The knowledge economy is not riding on rails; it's bouncing off satellites and inside cranial walls. The world is fundamentally a different place, requiring different beliefs and behaviors.

A directive management style may have worked in the industrial age, for a manager could observe whether someone was working and easily measure how much that worker produced. But think about managing knowledge work. It is much more difficult to measure. You cannot demand that someone have a good idea today; you cannot even tell if someone is working! The kick-butt-and-take-names management style clearly will not produce results when the primary transaction of work occurs within and between human brains.

The changes in our economy are also affecting customer expectations. In 1991, the Department of Labor and the American Society for Training and Development conducted a study to determine the new competitive standards, those factors that will drive success into the 21st century. They identified five competitive standards: quality, variety, convenience, customization, and timeliness.[8]

The relative importance of these standards will vary by industry and within industries. But all five factors are now more important than the ability to mass-produce products or services. In the old world, you could tell your customer, "Cheap, fast, or right. Pick any two." Now customers are demanding, "All of the above."

The situation becomes even more demanding when you consider the changes in demographics in the United States. With the baby boomers entering the job market over the past two decades, we have enjoyed an almost unlimited supply of increasingly skilled labor. And those individuals have been far less willing than their parents to take orders and be thankful for a job. They demand a say. If you don't like the demands of your existing employees, you can't just replace them with new ones. With the baby bust comes a dearth of skilled workers.

The bottom line is that you will need to work with the people you have, they will need significant and constant retraining, and they will demand to be involved in decisions that affect them.

Meditating on the New Economy

If your organization is still saying, "It worked for 30 years. If it ain't broke, don't fix it," your primary task is one of education. The leaders must understand the implications of a knowledge-based economy and new technologies for their organization. After reviewing some of the materials listed in the Recommended Reading section, we suggest this exercise:

1. Brainstorm the changes that are occurring in the following areas: society, your industry, technology, your competition, your customers, your employees, and other factors inside your organization.

2. Decide which of the trends will continue and which will reverse themselves (as with a pendulum).

---

[8] Anthony Carnavale, *America and the New Economy* (Washington, DC: American Society for Training and Development and U.S. Department of Labor, 1991).

3. Consider any radical, discontinuous changes that may be on the horizon, changes that are not a natural extension of an existing trend.

4. Extrapolate this information to create a picture of what your workplace will be like in 10 years.

5. Review every change you have identified, and begin listing things your organization must do to adapt to them.

6. Review the adaptations and see how many relate to self-direction.

NO LINK TO STRATEGY

So far in this chapter, we have dealt with complacency and misconceptions. Some organizations recognize the need to change and understand self-directed teams. Their problem is that they are not crystal clear on how self-directed teams will help them achieve their long-term strategies. Keeping company with this group are those who want to do teams because "they are a good thing to do." While it would seem odd if we disagreed with their basic premise, it is important to have a clearly defined need to change. The fact is, not everyone in the organization will agree that teams are "a good thing to do," and everyone will want to know why the organization should implement them. You had best have a clear and compelling answer.

Benefits of Teams versus the New Competitive Standards

Self-directed teams have been proven to offer numerous benefits to an organization. In his book *High-Involvement Management*, Edward Lawler shares the results of his research on a variety of employee involvement methods. While less aggressive forms of empowerment were not found to yield many benefits, self-directed teams improved many indicators, including quality, customer satisfaction, productivity, and safety.[9] According to Procter & Gamble executive Charles Eberle, these teams were found to improve almost every business indicator by 30 to 50 percent.[10] Within individual work areas such as the Consolidated Freightways

---

[9] Edward Lawler, *High-Involvement Management* (San Francisco: Jossey Bass, 1986).

[10] Kimball Fisher, *Leading Self-Directed Work Teams* (New York: McGraw-Hill, 1993).

example mentioned earlier (where cycle time dropped from five weeks to ten days), the improvements may be quantum leaps over previous performance levels.

It is not enough to be excited about these general motherhood-and-apple-pie benefits. Before implementing SDWTs, you should know exactly which elements of organizational performance you are trying to improve. This clarity will help you answer all the *why* questions the employees will ask and will also guide future decisions, such as how to restructure.

For example, one of us recently sat in on a design team meeting in which the company's marketing executive was delivering a briefing on future customer needs. We asked him, "The team will need to make trade-offs. If they could produce a design that would primarily improve product quality, cycle time, relationship with customers, or the variety of products produced, which would you choose?" His answer provided critical guidance for the team.

Consider the relative priority of the new competitive standards for your organization. Get consensus from the key organizational stakeholders about their ranking or relative weight. (See Chapter Four for information on how to organize teams to meet each of these competitive standards.)

Ask Not What You Can Do for Teams; Ask What Teams Can Do for You

There are many ways to decide what problems SDWTs should solve in your organization. Following is a structured way to arrive at a decision using common quality tools. The advantage of this approach is that for organizations interested in total quality management, the managers can model the use of the tools. This process is appropriate to implement after the members participating in the process have been educated about SDWTs and their benefits.

Interrelationship Digraph. Interrelationship digraphs map the relationships between various causes and effects. They help you get to the critical few root causes. Follow these steps:

1. Write this question on a board or flip chart: What problems are we currently experiencing (or are anticipating in the near term) that you think SDWTs could address?

2. Have the participants write their answers on adhesive-backed notes, one answer per note.

3. Place one note down and ask who else had a similar answer. Stack the similar answers on top of one another with a summarizing label on top (e.g., "lack of trust" might summarize many of the individual answers).

4. Repeat the previous step for another set of answers.

5. With only two sets of answers on the board, draw an arrow between them indicating which primarily leads to the other. Draw the arrow from the cause to the effect. Do not draw arrows in both directions!

6. Add another set of answers, and consider whether a relationship exists among the three sets of answers. Draw arrows as appropriate.

7. Continue this process until all the answers are on the board, making sure that each time you add a set of answers, you consider its relationship to all the other answers on the board. Using different-colored pens can help in interpreting the inevitably messy chart.

    If, after discussing the direction of the arrows, the participants still disagree about which way the arrows should be drawn—which is a cause and which is an effect—you should validate your assumptions with others before finalizing the chart.

8. When all the arrows have been drawn, count the number of arrows coming in and out of each set of answers. Those sets with the largest number of arrows coming *out* are the key causes. Those with the largest number coming *in* are the key effects.

Now that you know the key causes and effects, you should consider the importance of the effects. If the effects are not serious enough to warrant a major change effort, you should consider less disruptive approaches.

Take each of the critical causes and effects from the interrelationship digraph, and answer these questions:

- What does this cost our organization? (Estimate this amount in dollars, if possible.)

- What is the trend (is it going to get worse, get better, or stay the same if we do nothing)?

- What is the likely result if we do nothing (take no corrective action)?

We suggest breaking up into subgroups to do this analysis, assigning one effect to each group. Then have the subgroups report.

Now you should have quantified the cost to your organization of not having self-directed teams. Or, to look at it from a positive perspective, you have identified the potential improvement if you implement SDWTs. These data provide the foundation for writing a case for change.

Developing a Case for Change

Before deciding to implement teams, you should summarize your case for change in a report that includes these components:

- *The situation:* What is the organization currently experiencing from its environment (e.g., increased competition, reduced funding, hostile regulators)?
- *The problems or challenges:* What internal factors inhibit an appropriate response to the external situation (the effects from the interrelationship digraph)?
- *Root causes:* What are the primary causes of the problems (the causes)?
- *Ramifications:* What are these issues costing us, and what will likely happen if we do nothing to address them?
- *Expected results:* How do you expect teams to improve your ability to respond to your situation? List specific measures or outcomes you expect teams to improve.

This information should be placed into a report and turned into a presentation for all employees.

CONCLUSION

Many organizations fail with self-direction because they fail to get started with a solid foundation. To ensure that the effort will be supported, it is critical that the organization's leaders have a felt need to change, understand self-direction, and have clearly defined issues that self-direction can address.

RECOMMENDED READING

Drucker, Peter. "The Rise of the Knowledge Society." Spring 1993, pp. 52–76.

Fisher, Kimball. "Diagnostic Issues for Work Teams." In *Diagnosis for Organizational Change*, ed. Ann Howard. New York: Guilford Publications, 1994.

Hitchcock, Darcy. "Dorothy Discovers Three Levels of Empowerment." *Journal for Quality and Participation* 15 (October–November 1992), pp. 22–24.

Hitchcock, Darcy. "Overcoming the Top Ten Self-Directed Team Stoppers." *Journal for Quality and Participation* 15 (December 1992), pp. 42–47.

Katzenbach, Jon. "The Discipline of Teams." *Harvard Business Review*, March–April 1993, pp. 111–20.

Katzenbach, Jon, and Douglas Smith. *The Wisdom of Teams*. New York: Harper Business, 1993.

Kohn, Alfie. *No Contest: The Case Against Competition*. Boston: Houghton Mifflin, 1986.

Lawler, Edward. *High-Involvement Management*. San Francisco: Jossey Bass, 1986.

Peters, Tom. *Liberation Management: Necessary Disorganization for the Nanosecond Nineties*. New York: Alfred A. Knopf, 1992.

Walton, R.E. "From Control to Commitment in the Workplace." *Harvard Business Review*, March–April 1985, pp. 77–84.

Webber, Alan. "What's So New about the New Economy?" *Harvard Business Review*, January–February 1993, pp. 24–42.

Chapter Two

But It Sounds So Scary

F ear prevents many organizations from implementing self-directed teams. With downsizing, rightsizing, and delayering, managers already feel they should be listed as an endangered species. Many managers equate self-directed teams with career suicide. Many specialists and support employees such as engineers, human resource specialists, and lead workers have similar reactions, for self-direction often requires that they share their special knowledge, relinquishing a primary source of self-esteem and status in traditional organizations. Front-line employees frequently mistrust management's motives, and some are less than eager to assume leadership responsibilities. Unions may fear that self-direction is just a ploy by management to undermine their influence. It seems practically every person in an organization has reason to resist!

In this chapter, we discuss how to overcome each of these sources of resistance, for it is critical that people believe that SDWTs will be good not only for the organization (which we addressed in Chapter One) but also for *them*.

WEE-WILLIES OR BIG-WILLIES?

You may be wondering why you can't simply move forward implementing teams and address the issue of fear along the way. Unfortunately, it is easy to underestimate the degree of the resistance, for in a traditional organization, almost everyone has learned to smile and say "yessir!"

In 1992, Axis Performance Advisors conducted an Obstacles Assessment, which measured the relative strength of a variety of potential obstacles to self-direction. We surveyed over 200 people across industries. The number one obstacle was employees' mistrust of management's motives. This was closely followed by unclear expectations and resistance.[1] It is foolhardy to proceed without addressing these visceral reactions.

Every change, welcome or otherwise, brings with it a period of anxiety and a set of losses. It is important to help the various stakeholders in your organization through their personal transitions. Since people tend to prefer the devil they know to the one they don't, they may even resist changes that they view as positive. It is important to educate everyone about self-direction early in the process so they can begin their own personal transition.

FEARS OF MANAGEMENT

Linda Moran, a consultant with Zenger-Miller, estimates that self-directed teams have only a 25 percent chance of success if managers and supervisors are dead set against it.[2] Managers and supervisors play a pivotal role in the implementation, so ignoring their concerns is a recipe for failure. We know of at least one client that held a lively discussion around whether supervisors should even be included in the redesign effort. Fortunately, they decided the supervisors should. When managers and supervisors are properly prepared, they can provide most of the support necessary to manage the transition, so do not neglect their needs. You should begin the effort with two assumptions: There will be enough for everyone to do, and everyone's role will change.

Their Losses

At first glance, managers and supervisors have a lot to lose. First on the list are their jobs. When we define self-direction as the team sharing most—if not all—the responsibilities of a traditional supervisor, defensiveness on the part of first-line supervisors is understandable.

To confuse matters, many organizations have begun to implement self-directed teams by eliminating a tier of managers. One client retired almost all of its foremen within a year and created de facto self-directed teams. An even worse situation was created in one region of a transportation agency, where management used the implementation of teams as an excuse to deal with supervisors with chronic performance problems; they

---

[1]Darcy Hitchcock, "Overcoming the Top Ten Self-Directed Team Stoppers," *Journal for Quality and Participation* 15 (December 1992), pp. 42–47.

[2]Beverly Geber, "From Manager into Coach," *Training Magazine*, February 1992, pp. 25–31.

fired them. While over six years have passed, supervisors in the other regions still equate self-direction with the elimination of their jobs.

This approach has several problems. First, it creates additional resistance from people whose support you need the most. Supervisors are the ones who know how to do the tasks the teams will be assuming. If the supervisors are no longer around, the team has no one to show them what to do. In these situations, one of two things happen: Important work falls through the cracks, or the tier of management above the supervisors gets overloaded from being forced to assume any supervisory duties the teams are not ready to perform. In most cases, consistent with Murphy's Law, both happen.

The fact is, coaching a self-directed team in the first year or two is *more* than a full-time job. What supervisors do will change, but there is a great deal to keep them busy. Kimball Fisher, author of two books on self-direction, maintains that organizations that cut back management significantly eventually find their progress stalling. As he puts it, "Self-directed teams require a change in the management role, not an elimination of managers. Coaching teams is a full-time job."

Even if you convince managers that their jobs are not at risk, a host of other losses will surface. Their self-image as the people with the answers will be questioned. They may fear that they will lose control over the team but still be held accountable for the team's performance. Many secretly fear that they will not be able to perform in this new environment. With this new role comes a loss of competence and predictability. For some, a perceived loss of power and status is paramount. Fisher tells a story about a manager who reacted to his new role by blurting, "What am I going to tell my mother?"[3] While this may seem an absurd reaction, for this individual who had surpassed the educational and professional achievements of all other family members, becoming a coach represented a major demotion in the eyes of those he cared about most.

How to Help Managers Discover the Benefits for Them

The key benefits of self-direction for managers and supervisors can best be summed up by Eva Caradonna, a team coach and supervisor at an automotive plant. We recently asked her what it was like now that her

---

[3]Ibid.

teams are well advanced into self-direction. "It's great!" she said. "Now people bring me solutions instead of problems, and a lot of things they figure out for themselves." With a sigh, she added, " I don't have to be God anymore."

The role of a traditional supervisor is incredibly demanding. It requires omniscience; the supervisor is expected to always know what to do and to be right. At least for Caradonna, it's a relief not to have to fill shoes more fitting for a higher being.

Managers and supervisors need to hear this message from their peers. Executives and consultants can tell them, but peers are a more credible source. Take your managers and supervisors on site visits to other organizations that are further along in the process, and let them ask their peers the tough questions that are worrying them. In addition to site visits, orchestrate other opportunities for them to interact with their peers such as conferences and professional association meetings. A reverse site visit is also possible. For example, Boeing's sheet metal center in Auburn, Washington, flew in a panel of people from across the country to speak to their managers, and videotaped the event. Another organization created internal support meetings that it dubbed AA (Autocrats Anonymous) meetings.

Invite the participation of managers and supervisors at the beginning. Engage them in the organizational learning effort, and involve them in building the case for change (see Chapter One). Ask them what assistance they think they will need to make the change, and then provide the support they request.

Establish human resource policies for the change effort to address their fears about job loss, compensation, and developmental support. In particular, they will expect answers to these questions:

- What happens if what I do now isn't needed in the new workplace? Will I lose my job or be reassigned? What if I don't like my career options?
- What if the next position I hold is at a lower pay grade? Will I lose money or get "red-lined"?
- How long will I have to develop new skills, and how much support will be there to help me?

The question that you cannot and should not answer is what their jobs will be in the future. That they must figure out for themselves. Their future roles will be determined by their own interests and talents, the needs of their teams, and the needs of the organization. As Peter Block so aptly points out in *Stewardship,*

> When a level of management has to look up in the organization like chicks in a nest, and ask, "If I don't control, what's my new role? What's my new role?" the tough and honest answer is "If you're looking for us to answer the question for you, you may not have a new role." The fact that middle managers keep asking others to define their jobs is their recognition that they are an endangered species. If they have the courage, they have the capability to answer the question themselves, through dialogue and negotiation with those that report to them.4

You can, however, help them define a preferred future. Here is a process we like to use. It begins by creating a desire on the part of managers to free up their time and then shows them how to find the time:

1. Ask the managers/supervisors to imagine that you could magically free up 10 to 20 hours per week of their time. Have them list things they would love to do with that time that might add value to the organization. (Golfing doesn't count unless the organization is a country club or is interested in job sharing and part-time supervisors.)

2. Have the managers pick one option that most excites them, and help them write a business case for the idea: What is it? What would it take to do it (hours, support, cooperation from others, training, etc.)? What would the tangible benefits and payback be for the organization?

3. Have them list on adhesive-backed notes tasks that they regularly perform, and ask them to estimate the number of hours a week each task requires. If desired, they can log their time for a week or a month to gather data on their time use. This log is often enlightening, but not required.

4. Have the managers place the tasks on a grid with the following headings:

   - Low value (for tasks they should stop doing or reduce substantially).
   - Delegate to teams (for tasks the teams could eventually assume).

4Peter Block, *Stewardship: Choosing Service or Self-Interest* (San Francisco: Berrett-Koehler Publishing, 1993), p 106.

- Keep or start doing (for tasks they will continue to perform or need to begin doing, such as coaching the teams). They may need to add new tasks, tasks they are not currently doing, into this column.

5. Add up the hours in the columns to see if your managers have freed up enough time to assume the new responsibilities they chose in step 2.

6. Have the managers share their results and challenge one another's assumptions. Strive to free up enough time to enable the managers to take on their new responsibilities.

When done properly, this activity can generate a great deal of excitement. Some managers have come up with the idea of making their area a profit center and serving new customers. Others have decided to pursue areas of technical interest. Many take on problems that have vexed them for years. The point is to get them excited about the possibilities that more self-sufficient employees could offer them and then show them that, while it will take time, it is possible to free up the hours they need to do something new.

FEARS OF SPECIALISTS

The fears that specialists harbor will be similar to those of managers, but the emphasis will be on the loss of self-image and fear about becoming obsolete.

Their Losses

Many specialists hold a stronger allegiance to their professions than to their organizations. Their careers are predicated on knowing what others do not know. In many cases, they must share much of their knowledge with self-directed teams and must let go of the role of hero—riding in to save the day, leaving their co-workers to wonder, "Who was that masked man?"

For example, many maintenance workers get a thrill out of fixing broken equipment. The plant is in an uproar when they arrive, and after they perform their magic with tools, they leave the plant purring. Few specialists will admit to the rush their heroism brings; it's more acceptable to complain about being called in the middle of the night to rescue a computer gone awry or to resolve a labor dispute, but if you listen closely to their stories, you'll know the rush is there. In many cases, we are asking these hero-specialists to take off their masks, stay in town, and teach us how not to need them so often.

This loss of self-image is compounded in dynamic fields where a person's expertise can quickly become dated. If in your redesign you assign these people to the line teams where they report to managers who are ignorant of their professions, you must find a way for them to stay current in their fields. As Microsoft Manufacturing and Distribution discovered, it is not enough to encourage these specialists to meet occasionally. They need a technical leader to whom they can look for direction, consistency, and late-breaking news.

How to Help Specialists Discover the Benefits for Them

For many specialists, relinquishing the more mundane aspects of their work frees them to pursue their specialties in even more depth. These people find the transition relatively easy. However, some specialists really enjoy the simpler tasks of their professions and will miss giving them up. Of course, these individuals always have the option to follow the task into the team, but for many this is not an acceptable choice. And some, frankly, may be too arrogant to adapt.

Some organizations cut too deeply into specialized support areas, giving specialists reason to worry that the teams will miss important nuances. Just like the managers, they must let go over time and discover a new role for themselves. One such specialist described her own transition in this way:

> At first, I didn't want to give anything up. But then I gave up little pieces, I mean *really* little pieces, until I saw they [the teams] could handle it. Finally, I realized that I couldn't do everything I needed to do if I held on to all these tasks.[5]

Just as with managers, getting specialists to talk with their peers in more advanced stages of self-direction is helpful, so most of the recommendations for managers will also be helpful. Since the primary change they must make is one of self-image, however, it also helps to spend time

---

[5]Mark Brown, Darcy Hitchcock, and Marsha Willard, *Why TQM Fails and What to Do About It* (Burr Ridge, IL: Irwin Professional Publishing, 1994).

examining the effect their role would have on teams if they did not change. This process may help:

1. *Begin by validating the importance of their role in the old system.* Many specialists feel they are being told, "You've been doing it wrong all these years." Instead, you should reinforce how important their contributions have been in the parental organization.

2. *Discuss why the organization must change its mode of operating.* After the specialists are clear about why the organization must change, discuss how dysfunctional maintaining their existing role would be in the new system.

3. *Get them to envision what they would love to do if they could free up some time.* Complete a visioning activity similar to the one for managers in the previous section.

4. *Help them create a potential hand-off list.* Create a list of tasks they perform. Identify tasks that teams could perform with a little assistance and ones that the teams could perform independently with significant training.

5. *Work with them to prepare any needed training.* Involve them in the design, delivery, and follow-up of the team training.

FEARS OF EMPLOYEES

The biggest fear the vast majority of employees have is that self-direction is a Trojan horse, a great gift from a suspicious source. They fear that management is not really serious about sharing power and that implementing teams is simply a way to trick employees into doing more work for the same pay. Management capriciousness has been a primary source of contention since the dawn of organizations, and self-direction ups the ante. What management giveth, management may taketh away.

Their Losses

While many employees view self-direction with excitement, some will be reluctant to assume new responsibilities. This reluctance is usually driven by one of two factors. First, many employees fear what may happen when they make a mistake. Second, others have enjoyed the ability to complain without having to take responsibility for fixing anything. Such employees may lose their griping rights.

How to Help Employees Discover the Benefits for Them

Soon after exposing the organization's leaders to the concepts of self-direction, the employees should be brought into the process. Including them in site visits and conferences is helpful, but it is often impractical to send every employee off-site. Usually the most practical option is to provide all employees with an overview workshop early on. Since front-line employees often find outside experts a credible source of information and also judge management's commitment by expenditures, many organizations prefer to hire a consultant to do this training. The training should provide answers to these questions:

- Why is the organization considering self-directed teams?
- What are SDWTs, and how do they differ from other teams (such as quality improvement teams)?
- What are employees' rights and responsibilities in a self-directed workplace?
- What changes might they like to see in their workplace?

When we conduct this type of training, there are two cornerstones we consider critical. First, we go into the parents-or-partners discussion in some detail so that employees understand the responsibilities that come with the new rights. (See Chapter Six for more information on this.) Second, we have found that a simulation in which employees can see and feel the differences between a traditional and a self-directed workplace is important. Simulations can leave people with a rich and detailed understanding of these differences, and since the information is rooted in their own experience, it is credible. We have found our clients referring to the simulation years after the training was conducted.

FEARS OF UNIONS

Like employees, unions fear the Trojan horse. Unfortunately, historical precedence gives them grounds for their concerns. Workplace committees are an old and too frequently used strategy for avoiding unionization. Where the union already has a foothold, it sometimes views employee involvement as an attempt to shut it out on issues that overlap their territories. It is not likely to cooperate if it believes its usefulness is in question, and you will not get far without its cooperation. If your work force is represented by a union, the union must be included in the decision making from the beginning.

Their Losses

Unfortunately, some union officials have participated in the same selective responsibility that some employees do. For example, a tree nursery in the Pacific Northwest offered to open its books to the union, but the union initially refused to look at them. With knowledge comes responsibility. It appears the union wanted to continue to make unrealistic demands. Like employees, the union may lose griping rights.

In addition, some union officials have viewed their role as warrior against management. They know how to bargain and how to file grievances. They may not know how to cooperate. M. Scott Peck, best-selling author of *A Road Less Traveled* and *World Waiting to Be Born*, tells about a union-management negotiation session for a Fortune 500 company. The two parties agreed to work collaboratively as partners and were making record progress in reaching agreements and averting a potential strike. They felt obligated, though, to keep their compatible relationship a secret so as not to arouse suspicion. At one point in the process, a high-ranking union official announced a surprise visit. The negotiating team agreed to put on the show that was expected. They moved from the parlor room they had been using to a room with a long conference table. They dummied up stacks of official-looking documents and showed up for their performance with coats, ties, and stern expressions. "By the end of the morning the visiting official pronounced himself pleased by the progress of the proceedings" and left.[6]

We have also found that many unions are poorly informed about how the organization operates. We recall one plant chairman announcing that while the division was below budget, the funds would certainly be spent by year end. Strategic planning, budgeting, and other management rituals may be a mystery to unions. So to some degree, the union officials also face the same crisis of competence that the managers do.

Unions can be an incredible help if they are on board. In fact, a number of unions, including the AFL-CIO, the United Steelworkers, the Communication Workers of America, the Amalgamated Clothing and Textile

---

[6]M. Scott Peck, *World Waiting to Be Born* (New York: Bantam Books, 1993), p. 304.

Workers, and the Grain Millers, have publicly endorsed employee involvement and labor-management partnerships and advocated for these efforts in the organizations they represent.[7] In a division of an automobile manufacturer, we found many of the United Auto Workers representatives at least as heavily involved in supporting the implementation of teams as their management counterparts were. They withstood a lot of heat and expended extraordinary effort to help teams succeed.

How to Help Unions Discover the Benefits for Them

Rectifying long-standing adversarial relationships is beyond the scope of this book. If your union and organization are still operating under us–them rules, the place to begin is in building trust. For the purposes of this book, we must assume the organization and the union are at least on speaking terms.

Four approaches, pursued simultaneously, seem to yield the best results. First, the union must be accepted as a partner in the process. If management is the instigator of self-direction, it should go to the union very early in the decision-making process and ask the union to participate in it. Include the union in site visits and training. The union's right to exist and participate should never be questioned. See the AFL-CIO principles in Figure 2–1 as a sample employee involvement agreement between union and management.

Second, approach the subject of self-direction from the standpoint of values. If you examine self-direction from this perspective, the match between teams and what unions have always wanted is almost perfect. For decades, unions have wanted workers to have more input into their workplace, more control over quality, and more involvement in decisions that affect them. For decades, they have questioned the practice of evaluating individuals and having them compete for compensation. Self-directed teams acknowledge the validity of their long-held positions.

Many of the other positions that unions have been known for, such as narrow job classifications and an emphasis on seniority, are largely forms of protection against management capriciousness. For example, a plant chairman at a paper mill once remarked, "Of course, hiring will continue

---

[7]Commission on the Future of Worker-Management Relations, *Fact Finding Report* (Washington, DC: U.S. Department of Labor and U.S. Department of Commerce, May 1994), p. 51.

FIGURE 2–1
AFL-CIO Principles for Labor–Management Partnerships

First, we seek partnerships based on mutual recognition
and respect...

Second, the partnerships we seek must be based on the
collective bargaining relationship. Changes in work
organizations must be mutually agreed to...

Third, the partnerships must be founded on the principle of
equality. In concrete terms, this means that unions and
management must have an equal role in the development and
implementation of new work systems.

Fourth, the partnership must be dedicated to advancing
certain agreed-upon goals reflecting the parties' mutual interests.

Source: Commission on the Future of Worker-Management Relations, *Fact Finding Report* (Washington, DC: U.S. Department of Labor and U.S. Department of Commerce, May 1994), p. 50.

to be done on the basis of seniority; that is, until the employees have control over who is hired, and then they'll do it based on performance." We wondered whether he recognized the irony in his statement.

A third strategy is to allow the union to share as much as possible the responsibility of implementing the changes. Rather than sitting on the side and lobbing complaints and suggestions, make the union an active partner. At Miller Brewing Company in Trenton, Ohio, the union participated in management's weekly staff meetings to make decisions regarding operational planning and organizational goals.[8] At the Marion County Health Department in Salem, Oregon, the union conducted some of the initial training on self-direction. Involvement at this level almost ensures commitment to the long-term process.

The fourth important step is to spend as much effort helping the union redefine its own role as you do with managers and employees. Sometimes the source of funding for these efforts can become a barrier, but it is well worth the investment to keep the union in the same phase of development as the rest of the organization. Without this effort, you may find the union backtracking when employees and management are working well together.

---

[8]Ibid.

They must have established a compelling new vision for their role before grievances and complaints evaporate. (Edward Lawler's book *The Ultimate Advantage* has an insightful chapter on this topic.)

CONCLUSION

Because people don't readily admit to their fears, many organizations are unprepared for the trouble these feelings can cause. All organizations would be wise to expect at least some trepidation from their members and make efforts to surface and address it early in the process. Though the particular fears may vary from group to group, generally all can be allayed with reassurances and involvement.

RECOMMENDED READING

Belasco, James, and Ralph Stayer. *Flight of the Buffalo: Soaring to Excellence, Learning to let employees lead.* New York: Warner Books, 1993.

Bernstein, Aaron. "Why America Needs Unions, But Not the Kind It Has Now." *Business Week*, May 23, 1994, pp. 70–82.

Bridges, William. *Surviving Corporate Transition: Rational Management in a World of Mergers, Start-ups, Takeovers, Layoffs, Divestitures, Deregulation, and New Technologies.* Mill Valley, CA: William Bridges and Associates, 1988.

Klein, Janice. "Why Supervisors Resist Employee Involvement." *Harvard Business Review*, September–October 1984, pp. 87–95.

Lawler, Edward. *The Ultimate Advantage: Creating the High-Involvement Organization.* San Francisco: Jossey Bass, 1992.

Noes, David. *Healing the Wounds.* San Francisco: Jossey Bass, 1993.

Ryan, Kathleen, and Daniel Oestreich. *Driving Fear Out of the Workplace: How to Overcome the Invisible Barriers to Quality, Productivity and Innovation.* San Francisco: Jossey Bass, 1991.

Stayer, Ralph. "How I Learned to Let My Workers Lead." *Harvard Business Review,* November–December 1990, pp. 66–83.

Chapter Three

"They" Aren't Ready

M any organizations fail to successfully implement self-directed teams because everyone is waiting for everyone else to make the first move. Employees wait to see a sign from top management. Managers wait to see employees grab for more responsibility. Management and unions each wait for the other to drop their guard. The beauty of waiting for someone else, of course, is that you do not have to take responsibility for your own actions. That the other party isn't ready is a great excuse.

In this chapter, we explore the common beliefs about others that get in the way of moving forward. We discuss positive steps that everyone can and should take to improve the readiness of the organization. Also, since accepting responsibility is still a personal process, even in teams, we describe the stages people go through to become empowered and explain how to help everyone progress through the stages.

MANAGERS THINK EMPLOYEES AREN'T READY

Managers routinely underestimate what their employees can do. This lack of trust and respect is sometimes downright insulting. Recently, when one of us spoke to a ballroom full of managers about self-directed teams, one manager asked, "So what happens when you let the lunatics run the asylum?" A conspiratorial murmur swept across the room.

Few managers are so blatant in their disrespect, but their caretaking beliefs and manager-as-parent behaviors are slow to extinguish. Many managers simply cannot envision employees successfully performing many of their management tasks. These managers believe it is their role to do for employees what employees cannot do for themselves, and they believe the list is quite long.

Taking Off the Blinders

Sometimes the tasks managers assume employees cannot do are quite petty. A vice president of a large corporation solemnly told us that his division was already doing many of the things we had discussed. Later we discovered that the managers were afraid even to let the employees coordinate their own vacation schedules. While sometimes a contentious issue, coordinating schedules is *not* an advanced responsibility for a self-directed team.

Some managers (and employees) often confuse really good parenting with self-direction. Grateful and sometimes smug employees often tell us, "Our manager wouldn't think of making a decision without consulting us." This participatory style is often the most effective smokescreen for maintaining, consciously or unconsciously, power and control. You should see the brows furrow when we retort, "But would she let you make the decision by yourselves?"

Other off-limit tasks are more strategic in nature. In trying to avoid layoffs, one client decided to review the competitiveness of its benefits package to reduce labor costs. The human resources director worked with other executives to come up with a plan that seemed infinitely fair. To their dismay, employees and managers alike were upset about the take-aways. When we explored why employees were not more involved in the process, the answer was "Sometimes you just have to be the parent." We disagree.

Then there are the truly advanced responsibilities that employees in some organizations have assumed. For instance, at Johnsonville Foods, owner Ralph Stayer involved employees in a major strategic decision for the organization. They had the opportunity to take over production from a competing plant. Instead of making the decision with senior managers, Stayer took the issue to the plant floor. He explained the opportunity and asked employees to consider three questions: What would it take to do this? What could we do to lessen the risks? Should we do it? The employees came back with an emphatic "let's go for it."[1]

Semco in Brazil provides another intriguing example. This diverse organization weathered bankrupting inflation and unstable political environments to become an organization revered by executives, unions, and

[1] Ralph Stayer, "How I Let My Employees Lead," *Harvard Business Review*, November–December 1990, pp. 66–83.

employees alike. Semco has attained one of the highest levels of empowerment–organizational democracy. Many employees set their own pay.
They vote on major strategic decisions. In some cases, the employees
spin off their own operations to become entrepreneurs serving Semco and
others. They conduct appraisals on their managers rather than the other
way around, and, as owner Ricardo Semler, puts it,

> The results are posted for all to see. Does this mean workers can fire their
> bosses? I guess it does, since anyone who consistently gets bad grades usually
> leaves Semco, one way or another.[2]

Most managers cannot envision this level of responsibility. For more
information on advanced forms of empowerment, see Chapter Thirteen,
"Beyond Self-Direction."

Our Employees Are Different

Once exposed to this information, managers' next excuse is that it won't
work because "our" employees are different. Certainly being the most
admired organization in Brazil helps to recruit top talent. However, Semco
did not start out with this advantage. Semler built his organization largely
with the employees he already had. Sure, some executives couldn't make
the shift, but the vast majority of front-line employees stayed. The
employees were not the barrier to making this work.

A similar story is told about NUMMI, a joint venture between General
Motors and Toyota. Their phoenixlike resurrection of a plant prompted a
great deal of interest. When a group of managers was touring the facility,
they were overheard to remark, "But your employees are different." The
employees just shook their heads; they had been called back from layoff
to populate the plant. Eighty-five percent of the plant's work force were
the same employees who experienced punitive labor relations under a different regime.[3]

The point is not to malign managers; most are earnest and care about
their employees. The point is that managers must enlarge their percep-
tions of the capabilities of their employees. When asked, most employees
admit they could do more. Why aren't we letting them?

---

[2]Ricardo Semler, *Maverick* (New York: Warner Books, 1993), p. 7.

[3]Thomas Mahoney and John Deckop, "Y'Gotta Believe: Lessons from American vs Japanese
Run US Factories," *Organizational Dynamics* 21 (Spring 1993), p. 27.

Our Employees Don't Want More Responsibility

A small but significant minority of employees will say they do not want more responsibility. But only a few of them mean it. When the concept of self-directed teams is first bandied about, you will hear employees mutter, "That's what the supervisor gets the big bucks for. I don't want any part of this." They will ask if they will get paid more if they do the supervisor's job. They will express concern over what will happen if they make a mistake, and they will worry about the inevitable conflicts that may surface with their peers. The vast majority of employees, however, do want more control over their work, and their enthusiasm will be piqued when they begin to see the possibilities.

At an auto manufacturer where bad blood had flowed for decades, the employees were understandably reluctant to get more involved. Being "forced" to join a team became a contentious issue. In one area of particularly independent employees, about one-third of the "team members" were not attending meetings or getting involved. This situation remedied itself when the team began to build a business case for going to four 10-hour days.

In the past, management would probably have told them they couldn't do it, chalking it up to employee selfishness. In this case, however, management responded by laying out their boundaries. If the team could figure out a way to change their schedule without negatively affecting the company's costs or the quality of service they were providing, they could implement the four-10s on a pilot basis. The pilot provided a period to evaluate the results of the new schedule against the boundaries.

When uninvolved employees heard they might be able to get three-day weekends, they came running. Ultimately, the team found that by staggering the days they worked, they could actually *improve* customer service by offering more hours of service, making it easier for customers on off-shifts to contact them. While they may have been motivated by self-interest, they discovered a win–win resolution.

Positive Actions for Managers

The following six actions can be initiated immediately by any manager to lay the foundation for the implementation of teams:

- Educate yourself about extreme versions of empowerment to challenge your assumptions about what employees are capable of doing. Reading and site visits are the easiest ways to accomplish this. Share what you learn with others.

- Reassure employees that responsibilities will be delegated to them over time and with adequate training and coaching. Also reassure them that good-faith mistakes will not be punished. Be sure to demonstrate this promise at the first opportunity, as it may be hard for them to trust.

- Begin discussing undiscussables. In their book *Driving Fear Out of the Workplace*, Ryan and Oestreich found that management practices were by far the most common "undiscussables, " or, as they put it, "secrets that everyone knows." These undiscussables present barriers to open communication, problem resolution, and organizational performance. Since management practices represented 49 percent of the undiscussables (followed by co-worker performance at 10 percent), managers can learn a great deal about how to better lead their employees by beginning this dialogue.[4]

- In keeping with discussing undiscussables, ask employees direct questions about how you manage them. Clark Smith, manager at Fujitsu-ICL, asks: Is my style suitable for the work we do? Do you think I am capable of leading us toward greater excellence and opportunity? Have I helped you to achieve your personal goals? Do you trust me with our training plan? Am I consistent with the values I communicate and the decisions I make?[5]

- Enhance the trust and credibility you have with your employees by spending time with them. Like gravity, credibility and trust are inversely proportional to the distance between the two bodies. Pat Carrigan, the first woman to manage a General Motors assembly plant, said, "Earning credibility is a retail activity, a factory floor activity, a person-to-person one. It is gained in small quantities through physical presence." At the Lakewood plant outside Atlanta, her approach reduced grievances from an all-time high of 5,500 to near zero, and incidents of discipline declined by 82 percent. At another plant she managed, productivity rose 40 percent.[6] Trust and credibility pay off on the bottom line.

---

[4]Kathleen Ryan and Daniel Oestreich, *Driving Fear Out of the Workplace* (San Francisco: Jossey Bass, 1991), p. 31.

[5]James Kouzes and Barry Posner, *Credibility: How Leaders Gain and Lose It, Why People Demand It* (San Francisco: Jossey Bass, 1993), p. 214

[6]Ibid., p. 46.

- For one day or one week, keep a log of all decisions or problems your employees bring to you that you think they should be able to figure out on their own. This list, usually a long one, will provide you with a glimpse of just how dependent your employees feel and how much time this dependency is costing you.

EMPLOYEES THINK MANAGERS AREN'T READY

Just as managers question the readiness of employees, employees doubt whether their managers are ready. When we teach introductory seminars on self-directed teams, we are often asked, "This sounds great, but what do I do if my manager doesn't play along?" Front-line employees quickly sense the potential losses for their supervisors and expect resistance. What they may less readily sense is the degree to which their supervisors' past behavior was dictated by the system in which they operated.

One of our client supervisors was viewed as very controlling and demanding by the front-line employees, and many of them openly expressed concern over whether she could make the transition. When we shared this feedback with the supervisor, we learned that she did not enjoy the part of her job that required her to be the "bad guy." As the supervisor for customer service, where all customer contact was made, this supervisor became the lightning rod for all customer discontent. Her staff had no control over the resolutions that were handled in other sections of the organization. Her job was to relay customer complaints and ask why work had not yet been completed. The way work was designed forced her to be the "bad guy."

When they reconfigured the work around customers, assembling a cross-functional team to serve each customer group, not only was the supervisor able to relinquish her unpleasant role, but lost calls per month immediately dropped by 80 percent and customers were no longer angry about being kept on hold.

However, when you review the results of our Obstacles Survey (see Figure 3–1), you can see that employees have reason to be concerned. "Employees mistrust management motives" was the number one obstacle to implementing self-direction. Numbers three and four were "Managers and supervisors resist the change." Number seven was "Managers don't demonstrate participative skills." Number 10 was "Insufficient top management commitment." Many of the biggest potential obstacles rest on the desks of managers.

FIGURE 3-1
The Top 10 Obstacles to Self-Directed Teams

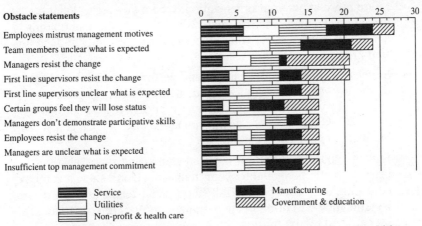

Obstacle statements

Employees mistrust management motives
Team members unclear what is expected
Managers resist the change
First line supervisors resist the change
First line supervisors unclear what is expected
Certain groups feel they will lose status
Managers don't demonstrate participative skills
Employees resist the change
Managers are unclear what is expected
Insufficient top management commitment

Service
Utilities
Non-profit & health care
Manufacturing
Government & education

Source: Darcy Hitchcock, "Overcoming the Top Ten Self-Directed Team Stoppers," *Journal for Quality and Participation*, December 1992.

Positive Actions for Employees

Many employees fear they will get their hopes up only to have them dashed. If they doubt the commitment or interest of their manager, employees are likely to settle for the status quo even when they see significant personal benefits in pursuing self-directed teams.

What can employees do to begin the process? According to Kouzes and Posner, authors of *Credibility*, most people seek the following characteristics in colleagues: honesty, cooperation, dependability, and competence.[7] Work to be better at all four:

- Make your manager's job easier. Talk to your manager about what he or she most likes and dislikes about supervising. Look for openings to change the manager's assumptions about what she or he must do. Identify any tasks your manager dislikes that might be interesting for you. Identify any tasks your manager might like to start doing if only the time were available (to give him or her an incentive to share responsibilities with you).

[7]Ibid., p. 255.

- Ask to take on additional responsibilities. Present a case for your idea that describes its benefits, its drawbacks, and your plan for mitigating the drawbacks, and then follow through.

- Learn more about your organization: whom you serve, what factors drive your business, what it costs to run it, what the future holds, and so on. Demonstrate your concern for the customer and the bottom line.

- Suggest ways to improve quality and performance while offering to do the legwork to carry out your idea. Avoid delegating the idea upward, or you will lose control over it and increase your manager's workload. Besides, asking someone else to fix it is just asking that person to be a parent.

- Educate yourself about self-directed teams, and share what you learn with others, including your manager. (Don't stage a coup by educating only your peers.) Talk about these teams in terms of the benefits they will bring to the organization first, to your manager second, and to you third.

MANAGEMENT AND UNIONS ARE SAYING, "YOU FIRST"

When unions are involved, yet another dance occurs. Management questions the union's readiness, and the union questions management's motives. Often they are locked in a stalemate, each waiting for the other to make a move. At LTV Corporation's new galvanized steel mill in Cleveland, the company struck a deal with the union: It would not try to keep the union out of the new plant if the union would agree to consider some new approaches. This new partnership gave employees the opportunity to decide how the plant would run in exchange for vastly increased flexibility in job classifications and other union rules. Management also agreed to let workers do the hiring as well as visit customers and select vendors. This new relationship was based on each side acknowledging the legitimacy of the other's needs and moving together on their common goals.[8]

These recommendations may help create a similarly workable partnership:

---

[8]John Holusha, "LTV's Weld of Worker and Manager," *The New York Times*, August 31, 1994, pp. C1–C4.

- Whichever side you are on, take the initiative. That's part of taking responsibility.
- Since differences often become exaggerated in front of an audience, begin with low-key, unofficial meetings at which trust can be built.
- Give the relationship time to develop. The other side will probably want to see you "make good" on new commitments before proceeding too far.
- Set some ground rules that will protect each side. Agree to confidentiality so that the participants will be honest. Make talking a no-risk situation by agreeing that the discussions will be exploratory and without obligation.
- Honor the needs or concerns of all players. Base your conversations on the assumption that all views are valid and legitimate.
- Focus first on areas where you agree, and work to uncover a higher common purpose.
- Begin documenting a framework for moving ahead that will protect the interests of both sides.

FIVE STEPS TO FULL EMPOWERMENT

The fact that everyone in the organization is *capable* of doing more does not mean they are *ready* to do more. Managers, employees, and union officials will be at different stages in their readiness. Their development tends to fall into five steps, as shown in Figure 3–2.

The analogies that follow are not meant to be interpreted literally; rather, they are intended to provide a frame of reference that may give you ideas about how to handle the situations. As you support others in their development, it is important not to resort to parent-child relationships. Approach the problems as you would with an equal partner by involving them in the decision making about what support they need.

FIGURE 3–2
Stages of Personal Empowerment

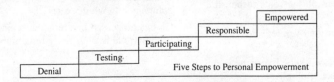

Denial is a bit like dealing with an alcoholic. Unless people stop enabling the person, he or she won't see a need to change. Managers who keep doing things *for* an employee or who shelter their employees from information, and employees who don't confront their managers on inappropriate behavior, are enabling the situation to continue.

If you are helping people through this stage, involve them in the educational process. Keep sharing information with them, invite them to attend site visits with you, send them copies of articles, and so on. Probe for their concerns, and accept any that have validity. Ask them what additional information they need to move ahead. Most of all, break the parent-child dependency. Explain why you cannot become a better parent, and instead emphasize why becoming partners is important for the future health of the organization.

Testing is like dealing with a preschooler. Here people test the boundaries, partly to see what they can get away with and partly to make sure the boundaries are still there. Employees may ask for "gimmes" such as four-day workweeks, day care, and the like. Disgruntled managers may try to sabotage the effort. One manager in state government threatened his employees with repercussions if they did not give him good ratings on his upward appraisal. To the organization's credit, he was removed from management within 24 hours and resigned within a week.

In the testing stage, clear boundaries and interim operating practices are helpful. Teams should be given specific operating guidelines and priorities. For example, in the benefits division of Consolidated Freightways, these guidelines were clarified in two documents called *Office Priorities* and *Office Boundaries*, which included the following:

Office Priorities	*Office Boundaries*
When we appreciate our customers, they appreciate us (customer service).	Customer satisfaction/customer loyalty
Answer the phone/answer the questions (customer service).	Phone coverage 6:00–4:30
	Minimal interruption of work flow
Whoever has the file owns it (claim ownership).	Reduce overtime
	Share responsibility
Yes—it *is* your job (personal responsibility).	In a team, but part of the office and the company as a whole
We are all starting over, let's do it together (new outlook).	Claims processed in a reasonable amount of time (goal is 5- to 7-day turnaround time)
Respect for co-workers. Everyone is entitled to be treated politely.	
Say "I will try," *not* "I won't" or "I can't."	

Furthermore, the responsibilities the team owns at any time and their degree of freedom should always be understood and negotiated. Frequently managers and employees think self-direction means all or nothing. In reality, there is a great range in the level of authority granted to teams. We describe this range in terms of "degrees of freedom." These degrees of freedom range from recommend, take action and notify your manager immediately, take action and notify your manager routinely (as in meeting minutes or monthly reports), and, as Nike's motto says, "Just do it."

Many managers have asked their employees to speak out only to be dismayed by their reluctance to participate. Employees may still look to the manager for ideas and guidance. Using structured and sometimes anonymous data-gathering methods can be a great help at this stage. Nominal group processes such as affinity diagrams (where individuals write their ideas on adhesive-backed notes, which are then posted anonymously on a board for analysis) force everyone to participate but protect them from any ridicule.

Participating is somewhat like the teenage years. These employees are ready to participate in decision making, but may lack all the skills and the confidence to make tough decisions on their own. Managers at this point are showing some willingness to let go of their responsibilities, but may still hover to make sure they are being done right.

When employees are in this stage, they may need Dumbo's feather. Dumbo, the big-eared elephant, thought he could fly because of a magic feather that he later discovered he did not need. Employees may need the same interim support mechanism. This may take the form of the manager participating in their decision-making process, providing them with worksheets, giving them a problem-solving process, and the like. The emphasis should be on doing new tasks *with* the team. This lessens the anxiety for both employees and their manager.

Responsible is like young adulthood. People have assumed responsibility for their own livelihood and are functioning quite well. However, they may not yet feel able to change the rules. "Responsible" carries a burden with it. Employees in this stage will function quite well, managing themselves in most situations. They may not, however, be proactive about influencing things outside their direct control. They may still accept the box they have been put inside. Managers in this stage will be taking direction from the team and operating as effective coaches. However, they may not have discovered a passion, something to do with their increasing discretionary time.

When both managers and employees have settled into their new responsibilities, visioning exercises can be helpful. Tap into everyone's personal passions to open new horizons. Ask thought-provoking questions to help them glimpse new possibilities, such as: If this were your business, what would you do differently? What would make this the perfect place to work? What organizational systems or policies prevent us from improving our performance? If we had to improve our performance by a factor of 10, what would we do differently? It's two years in the future, and you just overheard our customers raving about our new product or service; they can't believe they didn't think of it themselves; what is it?

Empowered is self-actualized. These individuals feel so much in control of their lives that they adapt their environment to suit them. They have the confidence to recreate their environment. George Bernard Shaw has been quoted as saying,

> Reasonable men adapt themselves to their environment;
> Unreasonable men adapt the environment to themselves.
> Thus all progress is the result of unreasonable men.

Forgive the non-PC language to share Shaw's insight. Empowered employees and managers can be "unreasonable" in that they feel empowered to change the size and shape of the box in which they live. They push against the system to make it more humane and workable.

When we were doing research for our last book, *Why TQM Fails and What to Do About It,* we found an example of this paradigm. We were interviewing Jerry Miller, who was then the personnel director at Brightwood, a small manufacturer of finished wood products in Madras, Oregon. Miller said that Brightwood hadn't fallen into the trap of we-work-for-the-customer thinking. This seemed an odd comment from the person who pioneered its quality effort. He went on to explain that the organization needed first to serve the employees and owners, since they had the most at stake. Delighting customers was a critical element in pursuing their own interests.

In the empowered stage, teams need more information about the organization, customers, and competitors. They should receive training in how to interpret financial statements. They can benchmark their performance against best practices. Encourage them to investigate new technologies and work methods. Teach them organizational development techniques such as re-engineering, process mapping, statistical process control, and the like.

CONCLUSION

No meaningful progress can be made on any change effort where deep-seated and secret doubts exist about any participant's ability to handle it. As with fear, these doubts should be surfaced and dispelled. Clarifying what the change means to each player and negotiating expectations is a good first step. This should be followed closely by demonstrated support and good-faith actions.

RECOMMENDED READING

Block, Peter. *Stewardship: Choosing Service over Self-Interest*. San Francisco: Berrett-Koehler Publishers, 1993.

Kouzes, James, and Barry Posner. *Credibility: How Leaders Gain and Lose It, Why People Demand It*. San Francisco: Jossey Bass, 1993.

Orsburn, Moran, and Zenger Musselwhite. *Self-Directed Work Teams: The New American Challenge*. Homewood, IL: Business One Irwin, 1990.

Thornburg, Linda. "Can Employee Involvement Programs Really Work?" *HR Magazine*, November 1993, pp. 48–52.

II

FALSE STARTS

O rganizations face many challenges early in the implementation process. Typically, few people in the organization have experience with self-directed teams. The leaders vested with the responsibility to implement these teams may feel like they have been asked to guide a voyage to Alpha Centauri. They don't know how to get there, nor what it will be like when they arrive. How can they know what to take, what to do, and how to prepare their passengers?

In *Chapter Four, "Where Do We Start?"*, we explain the implementation structures and process that are typically used. Then we cover the common mistakes organizations make early in the implementation. Some organizations mismatch their implementation strategy with their organizational needs, using too much or too little structure. Others try to lead the implementation by changing their compensation system. Many fail to consider whether their macro organization structure is appropriate for teams, assuming their existing departments will be the teams. Most neglect to plan a communication infrastructure to replace the traditional chain of command.

In Chapter Four, we provide concrete recommendations and examples for each of these problems. At the end of the chapter, we provide a detailed listing of steps you should consider in your implementation plan.

Once the broad, strategic decisions have been made, the organization must still decide how to translate the concept of self-direction into operating practices. In *Chapter Five, "Who Should Be on the Team?"*, we get into the nitty-gritty details. We explain the up-front analysis that should be completed before forming teams. Often this is done by a temporary task force of front-line employees called a *design team*. Whether or not a formal design team is chartered, whoever is charged with working out the details will share similar challenges. We address each of the common problems they will face and explain how to avoid them. We also provide a step-by-step listing of the tasks a design team should complete.

One of the most common problems organizations face is that everyone interprets self-direction to mean whatever they want it to mean. In Chapter Six, "Now We Can Do Whatever We Want, Right?", we address this phenomenon.

Self-direction can be deceptively intuitive. People often mistake the tangible manifestations of SDWTs for the essence of self-direction. They put small groups together and give them a little more power. But self-direction is not so much a structure or a set of responsibilities. It is a fundamentally different management philosophy, a different way of thinking about working together, with new rights and responsibilities for all. In Chapter Six, we explore the implied employment contract that self-direction represents.

In Chapter Six, we also explain some of the common problems organizations encounter when trying to empower front-line employees. To make sure no one drops the baton, we provide a worksheet to help you define the specific responsibilities your self-directed teams will assume. Managers need specific guidance about how to "coach" their teams, so we also provide guidelines and processes to help managers pass the baton to their teams.

Organizations tend to underestimate the amount of support required to implement self-directed teams. In Chapter Seven, "We Put You in Teams, So Why Aren't You Working?", we explain the necessary roles (i.e., champion, facilitator, and self-directed guide) and their associated challenges. Since managers are critical to the implementation, they require special attention. An entire section of the chapter is devoted to their needs and the barriers to their development. At the end of the chapter, we share the results of our research on what strategies are most effective in helping managers through their transition.

After reading Part II, you should have a thorough understanding of how to begin the implementation of teams. You'll be aware of the common omissions and mistakes organizations make, and you'll have a flexible yet structured model for planning your implementation.

Chapter Four

Where Do We Start?

F or many, implementing self-directed teams seems an overwhelming task. So much needs to be changed, and usually those responsible for implementing teams have little experience in doing so. It's easy for them to get stuck, uncertain of what to do when, and fearful of omitting important steps.

In this chapter, we will explore the common mistakes organizations make when planning the implementation of self-directed teams. These problems include mismatching the approach with the needs, leading with compensation, failing to revamp the organizational structure, and not providing for common team roles. Most of these issues reflect tasks that are performed by a steering committee. Specific omissions in the implementation process will be addressed in later chapters.

IMPLEMENTATION BASICS

Before we discuss the problems organizations encounter in planning their implementation of teams, it might be helpful to share with you the textbook approach to implementing teams. That way, you'll have something to compare the mistakes to. To that end, let's explore who does what and what gets done when.

Who Does What?

Most organizations use the structure shown in Figure 4–1 to manage the implementation. First, management usually appoints a *steering committee*,

FIGURE 4-1
Implementation Structure

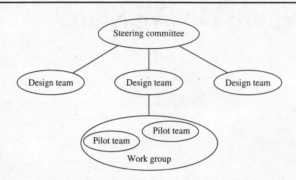

an oversight group with the clout to make teams happen. High-level managers of the affected work areas are included, as well as other critical stakeholders such as human resources, the union, future team members, and so on. Many organizations choose to pull people from all levels and areas of the organization, selecting them along a diagonal slice through the organization chart. This approach ensures thorough representation.

The steering committee should make as few decisions as necessary. It should focus on those issues that will need to be consistent across the entire organization. The details should be left up to the design teams or the work teams. The steering committee usually is responsible for these tasks:

- Making a go/no-go decision about implementing teams.
- Conducting a readiness assessment to determine barriers and areas where teams would be likely to succeed.
- Creating a broad implementation strategy (including whether to implement teams across the board or to begin in certain areas).
- Developing an implementation plan that includes resources for training, support, and the like.
- Chartering design teams to work out the details for their work areas.
- Monitoring the implementation and making appropriate mid-course corrections.
- Helping teams when they encounter barriers.
- Creating task forces to change organizational systems (compensation, purchasing, etc.) that present barriers to teams.

The steering committee charters one or more *design teams*, temporary task forces of front-line employees, to decide how self-direction will be applied in their work areas. The design team should also be a carefully selected group. Here it is important that members possess knowledge of the work to make the best decisions about how to staff and structure the teams. This usually implies a need for line workers from the affected areas as well as technical experts (i.e., engineering, maintenance). Like the steering committee, this group should maintain close connections to employees to ensure the design for teams reflects the needs and interests of the people who will staff them.

The design team should also make as few decisions as necessary. It should focus on those issues that will need to be consistent across its work area, leaving the work teams significant flexibility and power. Design teams are usually responsible for these tasks:

- Recommending improvements to the work process (e.g., eliminate steps in the process, purchase new equipment or technologies, improve physical layout).
- Deciding how many teams there will be.
- Defining roles and responsibilities for each team.
- Creating a process for assigning individuals to each team.
- Recommending changes to systems such as compensation, purchasing, and so on.
- Defining training and support required to get teams up and running.
- Creating a detailed implementation plan for their work areas.

Often the design team will charter one or more *pilot teams*, which are test sites for its recommendations. These pilot groups are initial self-directed work teams. Eventually, the entire work area migrates into these teams.

This chapter focuses on problems for steering committees. The next chapter covers the design team process and role in detail.

The Learning Spiral™: A Time and Place for Everything

The Learning Spiral™ is the model we use to help organizations plan the implementation of teams. It provides a structure that helps you know when to do what. By organizing the change effort, it also reduces the opportunity for omissions. We call it a Learning Spiral™ because it returns successively to certain tasks, each time performing the tasks at a higher level of sophistication or with a higher level of understanding. It also highlights the fact that the organization is embarking on a process of group learning. At the beginning, no one can truly envision what is possible. The organization must progress through planes of evolution, each time becoming better able to perform a more complex set of tasks. The Learning Spiral™ organizes the implementation into three phases (see Figure 4–2):

- Establishing a plan.
- Getting up and running.
- Aligning systems and linking to others.

Notice that the wedge to the left of the phases shows when the various structures (steering committees, design teams, task forces) are used.

In phase 1, executives and the steering committee establish an overall strategy and plan. In phase 2, significant time and energy are put into getting teams up and running. As these teams bump up against inhibiting organizational systems, the organization moves into phase 3. Leaving systems until phase 3 is important for two reasons. First, when you begin, you will not be able to forecast all of the systems that will need to be changed. Second, you will probably not be far enough along in your evolution to know how the systems should be changed. Remember, it's a *spiral* of learning.

Phase 3 is also the stage where the redesigned organization begins to reach out to educate others. By then the teams should have measurable successes that will help them weather the inevitable onslaught of naysayers.

Within each phase are four recurrent steps:

1. *Education and strategy*. First, people must educate themselves about the options and formulate a broad strategy for moving ahead.
2. *Leadership preparation*. Next, other important stakeholders must be identified and brought on board.
3. *Organization redesign*. Third, the structure of the organization or its systems should be examined and modified as necessary.
4. *Skill development*. Finally, everyone should be provided with the skills to operate within the new systems and structures in preparation for the next phase.

Each time the organization spirals through these recurrent steps, the focus changes. In phase 1, *establishing a plan,* the emphasis is on laying the foundation for teams. Executives must first educate themselves about

FIGURE 4–2
The Learning Spiral™

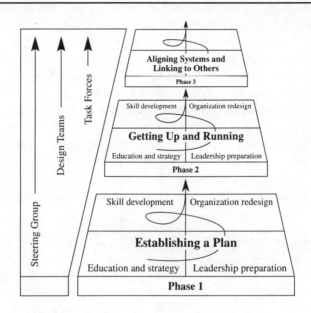

high-performance principles to decide how they mesh with organizational strategy. Then, as part of leadership preparation, other organizational leaders, such as union officials, human resources, managers, and supervisors may need to get involved. As part of organization redesign, the leaders may determine that the overall organizational structure should be changed to align with the team concept. This may require changing from a functional structure to one organized around customers or processes. Then the leaders must be provided with the necessary skills in preparation for the second phase.

In phase 2, *getting up and running,* the same four steps are revisited, but this time the emphasis is on working with front-line employees. Front-line employees must be educated, and those who will lead the effort must be prepared. Design teams are formed to redesign the organization in more detail, dividing into work teams and work cells. Then the team members must be given technical, interpersonal, and supervisory skills to function effectively.

Finally, in phase 3, *aligning systems and linking to others,* the organizational systems must be addressed. Many systems are incompatible with high-performance principles (e.g., compensation, performance appraisal, purchasing, goal setting) and need to be modified to allow the teams to succeed. Also, those who interface with the team (vendors, internal and external customers, support groups, etc.) must be educated about how the team is functioning and how these changes will affect them. Again, the organization must educate itself about the options, involve other stakeholders, redesign systems and relationships, and provide new skills.

Omitting steps is one of the most common causes for failure. In the appendix to this chapter, we include a detailed listing of what to do in each step.

Now that you know what the implementation process should look like, let's explore the common planning mistakes organizations make: mismatching their approach with their needs, leading with compensation, failing to restructure, and not providing for common team roles.

MISMATCHING THE APPROACH WITH THE NEEDS

Earlier we explained the textbook approach to implementing self-directed teams, including a steering committee and design teams. One approach does not fit all, however. Organizations that are implementing self-directed teams across the board will probably require a steering committee and will have to address many organization redesign issues. However, when managers implement these teams within an isolated pocket of the organization, less structure is required. We have identified three distinct implementation strategies: skill enhancement, integrated change, and work redesign.

Skill Enhancement

Some organizations can approach the transformation primarily through skill building. This strategy, the least costly of the three approaches, is most appropriate for small organizations or individual departments, where the rest of the organization may not be ready to embrace high-performance, self-directed practices. In these isolated settings, self-direction is driven primarily by management style. Most of the transition can be managed via workshops and training. Improvements and empowerment will be limited, however, because the rest of the organization may not be aligned.

Integrated Change

In many cases, it is wise to establish a cross-functional steering committee that assumes responsibility for overseeing the implementation and removing any systemic barriers. This approach facilitates the transfer of learning into other portions of the organization and helps maintain the momentum for change and keeps the effort visible. Steering committees require time and resources, but the payback is greater consistency across the organization and a more coherent implementation process.

Work Redesign

Forming design teams that re-engineer the work process usually yields the greatest performance improvement, since it ensures you are not designing work tasks and roles around an inefficient process. This approach is most appropriate when quantum leaps in performance are needed or you know that significant opportunities to improve the process exist. Changes in technology, a declining competitive standing, or benchmarking data can all imply the need for re-engineering a process.

Don't pick a more cumbersome and labor-intensive process than you need. If the team members are technically competent and possess good interpersonal and problem-solving skills, less up-front planning and analysis will be needed. The teams should be able to correct problems as they come up. On the other hand, if your redesign is likely to cross existing organizational boundaries, involve extensive capital, or significantly change the technical roles and responsibilities of the workers, design teams and steering committees are warranted.

LEADING WITH COMPENSATION

Recognizing that individualistic human resource systems are inconsistent with teams, some organizations begin the implementation by changing compensation. Since compensation is supposed to motivate, changing the system to support teams seems a logical first step. This is almost always a mistake.

The Problem with Bribes

One organization whose employees were represented by a union secured an agreement to implement teams at least in part by offering to increase their pay. (Recall that in the Learning Spiral™, changing systems is post-poned until phase 3.) Since teams are more productive, it seemed fair to pay them more. Also, increasing everyone's pay to match the highest pay grade was seen as a way to eliminate artificial status barriers between individuals. Immediately this change set off a firestorm of intergroup conflict. Certain groups, such as electricians, were accustomed to having more status and pay than other trades, so bringing everyone up to their level was a slap in the face. Why did everyone else *but* them get raises?

The second problem this approach caused was that people joined teams solely to get the extra money. These individuals showed up to team meetings and sat mutely with arms crossed, mocking the management give-away. They felt no obligation to raise their performance to earn the additional pay. Teams became a farce. While teams ultimately succeeded at this site, resolving these issues wasted valuable time in the implementation.

Another of our clients decided to implement a profit-sharing system to encourage employees to focus on the bottom line. Within a couple of months, executives were thrilled by the progress that had been made, and the employees' profit-sharing pool swelled to the equivalent of over two weeks' pay. Profits were up, and many changes had been initiated to improve short-term financial success. What was less readily apparent was the degree to which quality and long-term financial success were being hurt. "Empowerment" ran amok. People were heard to say, "What engineering standards?" and "The customer shouldn't notice." So-called improvements rapidly ballooned out of control. The employees did not have all the information, systems, and team maturity needed to work within the new compensation system.

Compensation systems should be changed. At issue is *when*. Done too early in the process, these systems distract people from the real task at hand: becoming more productive. They also prevent people from discovering the intrinsic personal benefits of joining teams.

The most damning condemnation of changing the compensation system first is that it is often done, or interpreted as being done, for the wrong reason: bribery. From the manager-as-parent paradigm, it is like bribing little Johnny not to cry at the doctor's in return for a lollipop. If you join teams, we will pay you more. As Alfie Kohn so powerfully presents in his book *Punished by Rewards*, traditional compensation systems reduce the intrinsic satisfaction people get from their jobs, lower the level of risk taking, and detract from the quality and creativity of the work. This is precisely what we *don't* want!

Why Compensation Should Wait

Compensation systems, along with other organizational systems, should be changed late in the implementation when they become significant obstacles to teams. Then everyone will better understand the partnering paradigm and will be able to design the new system jointly. Compensation should not be a bribe conferred to someone of lower status; it should be an equitable way to share the harvest. Until employees and managers alike understand they are working the fields together, they will not know how to share the wealth. (See Chapter Nine for more information on compensation systems.)

Lead with Symbols Instead

If you want to take a concrete action that demonstrates your commitment to partnering, destroy a symbol of hierarchy. One of our clients has a parking lot that is the epitome of class distinctions in traditional organizations. Along the entire length of two buildings is a row of reserved parking spaces for executives. (There are a lot of executives.) There are also a couple of short-term parking spots for short-term visitors (we guess they don't want you to stay long). Behind the reserved spots is the lot for nonunion (what they call "professional") employees. Beyond that lot and across the street, where the pavement is virtually gravel, is the lot for the union (unprofessional?) employees. So far, the executives have yet to see what's wrong with this setup. We hope they call us when they do.

When we needled another client about its reserved parking spots for executives, it dutifully painted over the names on the curb. Then it erected signs proclaiming, "Company vehicles only." Of course, only executives have company vehicles. We give up!

Every organization has these perks of status. If you want to demonstrate your commitment to partnering, management should give up something of substance. In one organization, we tore down the walls between the executive and employee cafeterias. In another, having managers wear more casual clothes was an "easy sell." In yet another, the plant manager moved his desk into the middle of the production floor. Honda America purposely didn't provide enough desks for the executives so that they would be forced to get out and talk with employees and customers.[1]

---

[1]Richard T. Pascale, *Managing on the Edge: How the Smartest Companies Use Conflict to Stay Ahead* (New York: Simon and Schuster, 1990).

Do something dramatic that shows employees the rules have changed. Give up something they think you cherish.

FAILING TO CHANGE THE MACRO ORGANIZATION STRUCTURE

Many organizations assume their existing structure is the right structure. In other words, they assume their existing departments will be the teams. Changing the macro organization structure may not occur to them until the teams encounter barriers caused by it.

The drawback to reorganizing after the fact is that the teams, having grown into cohesive units, will be even more resistant to change. Also, many organizations never address the issue of who should work with whom and so suboptimize the performance of the organization.

Functional ≠ Optimal

Unfortunately, most organizations are still structured functionally, putting people of like skills together. The problem with the birds-of-a-feather structure is that these people often are not interdependent. As we stated in Chapter One, teams should be formed with interdependent members.

Instead, many organizations organize around a process or a product, dismantling staff departments and reassigning certain members of MIS, accounting, maintenance, and engineering to the teams. This decentralization does not always make sense (as in the case where a team could not keep an engineer busy full time), but it should be considered.

Margaret Wheatley, author of the best-seller *Leadership and the New Science*, proposes organizing around information. Ask yourself: Who knows what I need, and who needs what I know?

How to Organize to Address Strategic Needs

In Chapter One, we discussed the new competitive standards that are defining success: quality, convenience, timeliness, customization, and variety. The relative priority of these factors will affect the structure and membership of the teams. The following guidelines are not hard-and-fast rules. The work and the workplace will pose some limitations. Also, these approaches are not mutually exclusive. However, you will probably never be able to maximize all five competitive standards with one design and so will have to make trade-offs.

Quality. If your primary goal is to improve the inherent quality of the product or service, it is critical to build a sense of shared purpose and goals among all the interdependent members who are involved with the design and production of the product or service. The best way to do this is to put them all on the same team. This usually requires dismantling the existing organization structure so that members of sales, marketing, and engineering, operators, buyers, and customer service representatives work together. A liaison with the customer who observes the use of the product or service is also helpful. Where forming such a team is impractical, a cross-functional oversight group should be formed to design new products/services and balance conflicting priorities.

Convenience. If your primary goal is to improve customer service, it is critical to build a link between the team and its customers. Instead of forming teams around process steps, consider forming them around customer groups. Someone on the team should act as liaison with the customers so that the feedback cycle is complete and immediate. As organizational boundaries blur, some teams even find ways to include the customer as a full member of the team.

Timeliness. If improving timeliness is your primary goal, focus on assembling a team with the fewest members possible to complete a whole process or serve an entire customer. Think small. When you perform a set of tasks on a small scale, many steps tend to be eliminated (such as sorting and hand-offs) and the work becomes easier to manage. For example, the Consolidated Freightways benefits teams no longer had to sort incoming mail, since each team had its own post office box. They didn't have to walk to a central filing area where files were stored by an arbitrary code; their active files were within arm's reach, a small stack that could be ordered in a manner meaningful to the team. And their customer base was small enough that the team members knew most of their customers by name, their case histories readily coming to mind.

Customization. Customization requires implementing the recommendations for both convenience and timeliness. The teams usually should focus on specific customer segments that share common needs.

Industry segmentation may not be as valuable as segmenting customers by needs. A county building department (which typically is divided into residential and commercial segments) could probably better serve its customers if it had different teams that served commercial developers, residential developers, contractors, and backyard do-it-yourselfers. These customer segments require vastly different levels of service. It might be possible to do only spot inspections of residential tracts on which the same structure is built with minor variations, whereas most backyard builders could benefit from a thorough education.

In some cases, a need for customization will require forming and reforming teams based on the needs of the project and the customer. In the facilities department of one major auto company, the carpenters, electricians, pipe fitters, and other trades were assembled into project teams based on the needs of the construction project. When the project was completed, they returned to the large pool to be reassigned. A cross-functional planning team was responsible for planning the projects, and a swat team of floaters handled ad hoc requests so that the project teams would not have to interrupt their jobs.

Variety. If your customers demand such a wide variety of products or services that it is impractical to have a team proficient in all, a front-office/back-office structure often works best. The "front" part of your process, the part that has direct contact with the customer, should be organized by customer segments so that the customer has a clear point of contact, someone who has a holistic view of its needs. The "back" part of the business process should be organized by products or services so that they can be delivered efficiently and the teams can specialize in certain products or services. In effect, the customer contact employee serves as a liaison with the "back office."

One example of where this approach should be applied is in government services. Most agencies have been formed around programs. The problem is that many people need multiple services and must run the rat's maze of bureaucracies. In *Reinventing Government*, the authors describe a teenage single mother with a juvenile record who had a half-dozen caseworkers, each presumably concerned only with his or her pound of her flesh. Contrast this with the approach Michigan tried to implement. Michigan's Job Training Coordinating Council invented the idea of an Opportunity Card, a credit card of sorts that would give every citizen access to services through the state. The plan was for a citizen to go to the

Opportunity Office (the front office), where a counselor would swipe the card through a reader and pull up information from the Human Investment database. The counselor would then refer the citizen to the specific services she or he needed (the back office).[2]

NOT PROVIDING FOR COMMON TEAM ROLES

Another common mistake organizations make is failing to establish a team-based communication structure, a function that is handled by the chain of command in traditional organizations. Instead, they let a structure emerge that often lacks the functionality of one planned in advance.

Role Proliferation

As teams assume supervisory responsibilities, they find it necessary to chunk them into logical roles. If an organization has not established a core set of common roles, teams will inevitably come up with different ways to share these responsibilities. Allowing these roles to develop ad hoc gives teams significant flexibility, but also presents two problems. First, without a common set of roles and responsibilities, training for these roles is almost impossible to systematize, increasing the already substantial training costs. Second, if teams do not have common roles, it is more difficult to link teams in a meaningful way and address common needs and problems.

Stars and Co-stars

The solution is to establish a set of critical roles that all teams will be expected to fill. Teams can always establish additional roles, of course, but core roles should be set up for responsibilities that fit these criteria:

- Tasks that will require significant training because they require advanced skills, involve legal risk, or change frequently (e.g., changes in environmental standards, human resource laws, software upgrades).

---

[2]David Osborne and Ted Gaebler, *Reinventing Government* (Reading, MA: Addison-Wesley, 1992).

FIGURE 4–3
Integrated Team Structure

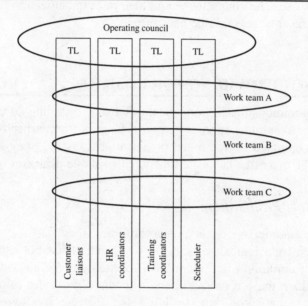

- Tasks that involve points of interdependence across teams where efforts need to be coordinated (e.g., job standards, scheduling, training, goal setting).
- Tasks that present significant opportunities for the teams to learn from one another (e.g., quality/process improvements, safety, customer contacts).

Many companies refer to these common roles as "star points" and rotate individuals through the roles on a periodic basis (with six months being a common term). Star points usually include a team leader/meeting facilitator, scheduler, and coordinators for safety, quality, training, and team administration. Some organizations find it helpful to have understudies who work with the existing star point to learn the role and fill in when he or she is not around. At Alliant Techsystems' Marine Systems group, a defense technology manufacturer in Mukilteo, Washington, they called one of these roles "co-stars."

These star points handle special leadership tasks for the team and usually run portions of the team meetings. They should also be expected to meet periodically with their respective star points from other teams. These cross-functional teams can resolve interteam problems, promote cooperation and learning, and establish consistent standards where needed. They should also be led by a technical expert in their star point (a safety manager, human resources director, etc.), someone who has the clout to enforce the standards and can bring the most current information to the team.

These interlocking work teams and specialist teams provide a practical communication infrastructure that supplants one of the primary roles of traditional supervisors. For example, in Figure 4–3, each work team has four specialist positions or star points: a customer liaison, a human resource coordinator, a training coordinator, and a work scheduler. In addition to handling leadership functions for their teams, these individuals meet periodically with star points from other teams to learn from one another and share resources. Each of these specialist teams has a team leader who sits on an operating council, which is responsible for making operating decisions and balancing the conflicting needs of the teams.

CONCLUSION

Many organizations concerned about the commitment and expense associated with the implementation of self-directed work teams try to take a casual approach. While this approach frequently results in some incremental gains, it is difficult to achieve the full potential of teams without a well-thought-out and officially sanctioned plan. This chapter provides such a plan. While any plan will need to be tailored, be sure to give careful consideration to all the issues mentioned here rather than underestimate the importance of any one of them.

RECOMMENDED READING

Hammer, Michael, and James Champy. *Reengineering the Corporation: A Manifesto for Business Revolution.* New York: Harper Business, 1993.

Hitchcock, Darcy, and Linda Lord. "A Convert's Primer to Socio-Tech." *Journal for Quality and Participation* 15 (June 1992), pp. 46–57.

Holpp, Lawrence. "Five Ways to Sink Self-Managed Teams." *Training* 30 (September 1993), pp. 38–42.

Kolodny, H.F., and B. Dresner. "Linking Arrangements and New Work Designs." *Organizational Dynamics* 14, no. 3 (1986), pp. 33–51.

Larson, Carl E., and Frank M. J. LaFasto. *Teamwork: What Must Go Right/What Can Go Wrong*. Newbury Park, CA: Sage Publications, 1989.

Orsburn, Moran, and Zenger Musselwhite. *Self-Directed Work Teams: The New American Challenge*. Homewood, IL: Business One Irwin, 1990.

Pasmore, W. A., *Designing Effective Organizations: The Sociotechnical Systems Perspective*. New York: John Wiley & Sons, 1988.

Shonk, James. *Team-Based Organizations: Developing a Successful Team Environment*. Homewood, IL: Business One Irwin, 1992.

Weisbord, Marvin. *Productive Workplaces: Organizing and Managing for Dignity, Meaning and Community*. San Francisco: Jossey Bass, 1987.

Appendix
Key steps in the Learning Spiral™

The following tables summarize the key steps you should complete in each step of the Learning Spiral™.

Phase 1: Establishing a Plan

Education and Strategy	Leadership Preparation	Organization Redesign	Skill Development
1. Familiarize executives with high-performance principles and issues. 2. Establish a basic implementation strategy (clarify strategic issues to be addressed by teams, scope, timing, structure, etc.).	3. Involve and educate other leaders (e.g., union officials, managers; set up steering committee if appropriate). 4. Enhance the plan (write case for change, conduct readiness assessment, responsibilities list, etc.).	5. Evaluate appropriateness of macro organizational structure. 6. Define and implement any needed restructuring (e.g., moving from functional to process-based structure).	7. Define future role of management and prioritize skill needs. 8. Begin leadership development.

Phase 2: Getting Up and Running

Education and Strategy	Leadership Preparation	Organization Redesign	Skill Development
1. Familiarize all employees with high-performance principles and issues. 2. Enhance the plan (e.g., decide on whether to use design teams, pilot groups; conduct a training needs assessment).	3. Prepare leaders to support the change (e.g., work redesign training for design team, more management development). 4. Prepare team members (e.g., provide awareness training on design team tasks, preparatory training on conflict management).	5. Analyze the workplace and recommend improvements (e.g., the design team tasks). 6. Implement optimal solutions (reorganize into work teams and implement new work processes).	7. Prepare teams to work together (develop team agreements and mission, identify customers and measures; select people to fill meeting and leadership roles; etc.). 8. Enhance skills of teams and their leaders (train intact teams on team skills and implement technical cross-training).

Phase 3: Aligning Systems and Linking to Others

Education and Strategy	Leadership Preparation	Organization Redesign	Skill Development
1. Identify needed system changes (i.e., human resource, financial, information, and planning systems). 2. Begin researching best practices and educating other groups.	3. Involve and educate other leaders/stakeholders. 4. Establish priorities and a plan.	5. Form task forces to recommend changes to organizational systems. 6. Implement optimal solutions.	7. Train organizational members in new systems. 8. Reach for the next level of performance through innovation diffusion and renewal.

Chapter 5

Who Should Be on the Team?

T ranslating the theory of self-direction into specifics is fraught with potential problems. Someone must decide how many teams there will be and who should be on each team. Someone must also decide what preparation the team will need and develop a detailed implementation plan. As usual, the devil is in the details.

To answer these questions, most organizations form a design team, a temporary task force chartered with the responsibility to figure out how the concept of self-direction will be applied in their workplace. Composed primarily of front-line employees with little or no experience in work redesign, these design teams typically struggle.

Even when a design team is not formally created, someone fulfills its task. Whoever completes the detailed work redesign will likely encounter several struggles. First, these individuals usually have no experience in work redesign and so are often confused about their task. Second, they often hold an inappropriate concept of their role, believing their job is to decide on behalf of their co-workers. Third, since they have been asked to complete an imposing task, they often lack confidence and need support throughout the design team process.

After explaining what a design team is and what it does, we will discuss each of these causes of failure.[1]

WHAT DOES A DESIGN TEAM DO?

Design teams are usually chartered by a steering committee or management team to make detailed recommendations about how to redesign their work around self-directed teams. While the steering committee makes

---

[1]This chapter is adapted from Darcy Hitchcock, "Think of Your Design Team as the Lead Raft," *Journal for Quality and Participation* 17 (July–August 1994), pp. 6–10.

decisions concerning issues that must be consistent across the organization, the design team makes decisions for its portion of the organization, often representing a department or work process. The design team should be composed primarily of front-line employees.

The Standard Approach

Most design teams follow some version of a sociotechnical systems (STS) design process in which both the social and technical aspects of work are analyzed and optimized. This involves reviewing and improving the technical aspects of the work such as work process, methods, technology, and physical layout. It also includes reviewing and improving the social aspects of work such as team structure, roles and responsibilities, reward systems, and group norms. Ultimately, the team must generate recommendations that represent an optimal balance between the needs of the work and those of the worker.

Here are some of the decisions and recommendations design teams are usually chartered to make:

- Recommend improvements to the work process (eliminate steps in the process, purchase new equipment or technologies, improve the physical layout, etc.).
- Decide how many teams there will be.
- Define common roles and responsibilities for each team.
- Create a process for assigning individuals to each team.
- Recommend changes to systems such as compensation, purchasing, and so on.
- Define training and support required to get teams up and running.
- Create a detailed implementation plan.

The Search Conference Option

The traditional STS approach takes time—usually 6 to 18 months, depending on the degree of detail. Some organizations have been experimenting with using Marvin Weisbord's future search conference structure as a way to increase involvement and reduce the time required. This approach involves conducting several large "conferences." The first conference focuses on identifying the strategic needs of the organization and includes representatives of all stakeholders (employees, management, customers, etc.). The second conference takes on the first design team task of analyzing the work flow and identifying improvements to the technical work system. The third focuses on the social/human issues such as structure and roles.

This approach is relatively new, but for those who have used it, it seems to significantly fast-forward the process. The drawback to this approach is that it often yields less radical changes. The benefit is that you can often involve all employees in the redesign effort.

Whether or not a design team is formed, whoever makes these decisions will face similar problems: how to get employee commitment to the redesign; how to make these decisions with little or no previous experience in work redesign; how to decide what to leave to the discretion of each team; how and how much to communicate with other groups such as the steering committee, other employees, and so on; and how to avoid analysis paralysis. The following sections cover the root causes of these problems: unfamiliarity with tasks, inappropriate roles and involvement, and low confidence.

UNFAMILIARITY WITH TASKS

Usually no one on the team has been on a design team before. In effect, team members have embarked together on a hazardous journey without a map. One solution, of course, is to provide them with a guide, someone with expertise in work redesign. However, they may rely too heavily on the expert and never assume responsibility for their tasks. This inhibits their commitment and contributes to low confidence. What the team needs is Dumbo's feather, something tangible to hang onto that will give them the courage to fly solo or at least with minimal assistance.

A Step-by-Step Process for Work Redesign

Since the design team members are unfamiliar with their task, provide them with a suggested set of steps and techniques so they don't waste valuable time. For example, *The Work Redesign Team Handbook: A Step-by-Step Guide to Creating Self-directed Teams*[2] shows teams how to complete these eight steps:

---

[2]Darcy Hitchcock, *The Work Redesign Team Handbook: A Step-by-Step Guide to Creating Self-directed Teams* (White Plains, NY: Quality Resources, 1994).

1. *Get ready.* The design team should establish a charter or mission that defines the team's purpose, outcomes, and constraints. It should also establish meeting ground rules and a plan for completing its tasks. This plan should include steps for educating and communicating with its own work groups as well as with other departments or parties that may be affected by the redesign. Team members should also be briefed on the strategic needs of the organization and its customers.

2. *Conduct a technical analysis of the work.* The design team should next examine the existing work flow and process, identifying opportunities to improve the efficiency and quality of the work. Root causes of common quality problems should be examined. This step may include diagramming the process, diagramming the work flow on a site plan, identifying technological options, and so on. Possible improvements to work methods, process, physical layout, and technology should be identified.

3. *Conduct a social analysis.* The design team should then examine the human aspects of its work. This step may include diagramming the team's network, examining potential role changes (combining jobs, cross training, etc.), and assessing employee satisfaction, as well as analyzing existing group norms, practices, and reward systems. From this analysis the design team should develop several structural options, including changes to positions (e.g., the elimination or combining of positions) and special roles (team leader, quality coordinator, etc.).

4. *Select the best combination of technical and social changes.* The design team should analyze the options derived from its technical and social analyses, testing them to the fullest extent possible. Then it should select the options that optimize social and technical needs. This should result in a diagram of team boundaries that includes the number and types of positions on each team. The design team should seek approval for these initial recommendations.

5. *Formalize the recommendations.* Once the basic design is approved, the design team should add detail to it. This may include writing job descriptions for new roles, identifying cross-training needs and levels, recommending a selection process for special roles (e.g., will they rotate, how often, who is eligible?), and deciding how teams will be formed (i.e., will people sign up or be assigned to the new teams?). An implementation timetable should be established.

6. *Identify related changes.* The design team must next consider what other changes should be made to support the new teams. This may include changes to human resource or business systems (e.g., implementing a pay-

for-skill compensation system, or negotiating a change in the purchasing procedures). The design team should also identify the resources they will need to carry out their plan (training, meeting space, status boards, new equipment, etc.).

7. *Troubleshoot the plan.* Before "going live," the design team should troubleshoot its plan. This may include brainstorming potential problems and solutions, as well as conducting a dry run of the new organization. This dry run should test, among other things, how the work teams will interface with other work groups, suppliers, and customers. Appropriate revisions to the plan and the design should be made.

8. *Develop a detailed implementation plan.* The design team should communicate with any affected parties outside of its work area and develop methods for supporting the implementation and resolving the problems that will inevitably occur. Any needed changes to policies or procedures that will be necessary for immediate operation should be completed.

Problems of Order

As we have mentioned and as the above process implies, the technical analysis of the work should come before the social analysis of the workplace. Organizations that do these steps in the reverse order or forget to do the technical analysis at all are likely to build inefficiencies into their new design.

The best way to explain this is to share with you a simulation we use in our workshops. Enlightened Industries, a simulated organization, makes paper lanterns. The assembly line process involves cutting a piece of 8.5″×11″ paper into a square, folding it into a lantern, coloring part of the lantern, and then unfolding two sides to create the final product. Since you can't add quality back into any process, the initial cutting step is critical. If the paper isn't square, all other steps in the process will suffer.

After becoming familiar with the process, participants are asked to redesign Enlightened Industries. Some teams omit the technical analysis and focus immediately on roles and structure. They usually come up with teams that complete a whole lantern, with all four steps represented. Some teams determine that the cutters need more training or better equipment like paper cutters instead of scissors.

Their faces usually fall when another team reports its suggested redesign. Teams that begin with the technical analysis quickly decide they should buy precut paper from the vendor, eliminating an entire step. Their cutters are retrained to perform some of the other steps in the process. These teams get better performance out of their employees, avoid additional capital expenses, and get better raw materials (since the vendor has access to a high-tech paper cutter). Also, by eliminating a step in their process, they have bought themselves some breathing space—the open space in the tile game—to make more improvements and conduct cross-training. The technical analysis is apt to make people question existing roles and responsibilities, leading to more radical improvements.

The one problem with doing the technical analysis first is that psychology is against you. Employees will want to discuss human issues first, before they will be ready to discuss the work process. This is the WIIFM principle: people want to know first, What's In It For Me? The following suggestions may help:

- Explain the design team steps to employees, and provide them with some initial training (including a simulation like Enlightened Industries) so they will understand the need to do the technical analysis first.
- Gather employee gripes and suggestions on both the technical and social aspects simultaneously.
- Move rather quickly through the initial social and technical analysis to initial recommendations. When people see what is being decided, they are more likely to speak up.

Direction from the Steering Committee

Management or the steering committee must establish the purpose of the design team and provide direction. Frequently, either through lack of foresight or a desire to empower the design team, management is reluctant to establish boundaries for the team. The design team is told, "The sky is the limit; we're willing to review any recommendations." Often the team's first proposals are quashed by management after the team spent many meetings grappling with the issues and generating enthusiastic consensus for its recommendations. Needless to say, this saps the enthusiasm of the design team members.

Before a design team is formed, managers should provide written answers to these questions:

- What is the *purpose* of the design team? Why is it being formed? Specifically, what business issues is it hoped their redesign will

address (e.g., quality problems, poor employee morale). Estimate
the current cost of those problems or lost opportunities.

- What are the *constraints* or boundaries on the design team? How
  often can it meet? Does it have a budget? To whom can it talk? Are
  there systems or work groups that are off limits? What can the team
  decide, and what can it only recommend? What criteria should be
  used to evaluate the team's ideas? What are its deadlines? Can
  members work overtime? What resources does the team have at its
  disposal?

- What are management's *expectations* for the design team? How
  often should the team report to management or the steering committee? How much time outside of meetings can it spend on design
  team business and analysis? Is there a basic process you expect the
  team to follow, and should the team emphasize certain aspects of its
  analysis more than others? How much is the team expected to
  involve the employees it represents?

- What are the *"givens"*? For example, has a list of team responsibilities been drafted by management? Are there certain roles that all
  teams must have to facilitate communication across teams? Is a
  gain-sharing compensation system already in the works?

- What is the *composition* of the design team, and how will its members be selected? Ideally, the employees should be allowed to nomi-
  nate people to the design team. You might also consider involving
  someone from outside the represented work group who can challenge the group's assumptions about the way the work should be
  done. If employees select their own representatives, they should
  understand what the design team will be asked to do and be given
  some guidance about criteria to consider (e.g., technical expertise,
  communication skills, leadership ability, and willingness to challenge the status quo). The design team should also represent a balance of men and women, races, tenure, and other factors.

Answers to these questions will spare the design team lots of time and
frustration.

INAPPROPRIATE ROLES AND INVOLVEMENT

Most problems during the design phase stem from inappropriate roles:
The design team members are often led to believe they should make all
the decisions for their peers; managers tend to meddle or abdicate; and
some organizations confuse pilot groups and design teams.

Who's in Charge Here?

Design teams are often led to believe their role is to make decisions *for* their teammates. This causes several problems. First, it drives a wedge between the design team and the rest of the employees. The majority of the employees will still feel like powerless marionettes, but now, instead of management pulling their strings, their design team members are. In one organization, the design team members were called "minimanagers," and this was not intended as a compliment.

Also, if the design team meets in isolation for six months, members will be in a very different place in their development than their peers. They will find themselves trying to sell their recommendations to resistant employees. Design team members acting as representatives for other employees can also cause problems from a legal standpoint. This last issue is covered in detail in Chapter Ten, "Close Encounters with the Law."

Design Team as Tour Guide

Rather than viewing itself as the deciding body, a design team is better off viewing itself as a tour guide. Good tour guides seek to understand your interests and then identify interesting places to go and things to see. They explain what you should do before the trip and what you should take with you. They help you understand what you are seeing and experiencing. Tour guides do a lot of the tedious analysis and planning for you. Most of all, tour guides recognize that they cannot take your trip *for* you.

Design team tour guides take the rest of their work group with them on their journey. Rather than focusing on communicating what they have decided, design teams should focus on educating their co-workers so that they can give reasoned input and will have the same time to make their personal transition. The design team should involve co-workers at every step in the process, making them feel as if the design team is working for them, not vice versa. The design team should do everything it can to make sure its recommendations represent the collective will and commitment of the entire work group. Its job is not to communicate; it is to educate!

Decide as Little as Possible

One principle of sociotechnical systems (STS) design is called "minimum critical specifications." This high-fog factor term simply means that what is truly critical should be specified and made consistent for all teams.

The rest should be left to the discretion of the team and its members. Just as the steering committee makes as few decisions as necessary—only those that must be consistent across the organization—the design team should make only decisions that must be consistent across the work teams. This ensures that the teams will retain the maximum flexibility and power possible. Explaining this concept will also help reduce anxiety with the work group. All the employees can help decide what should be consistent across all teams.

The Role of the Manager on the Design Team

Managers also struggle with their role. They have a tendency to abdicate their responsibility to the design team, unsure of how to participate without controlling. Managers often decide not to attend team meetings. They wait for the design team to come to them with recommendations or problems. However, since the teams still have one foot in their traditional, autocratic workplace, they are not ready to travel this road alone. They need a coach, someone to observe their team process and provide critical input.

When managers do participate on the design team, they often end up running the meetings and monopolizing the process. If a manager is an excellent facilitator, taking the lead in managing the process is often helpful. However, most employees will tend to weight what their manager says too heavily and may feel as if the design team process is really the boss's show.

One alternative is to have managers sit in on the design teams as non-voting coaches. Their role should be clearly defined, just as the meeting facilitator's and recorder's roles are. Some of the coach's responsibilities include

- Helping the meeting facilitator plan the agenda.
- Helping the facilitator select and use appropriate analytical and group decision-making tools such as process diagrams, force field analyses, and so on.
- Observing the meeting and sharing observations about the group process.
- Interjecting information that the design team does not have.

- Helping the team build convincing proposals and recommendations.
- Gathering data for the team as requested (e.g., getting quotes from equipment manufacturers and researching appropriate training opportunities).
- Generating support for the team's recommendations and ideas with powerful members of management, union officials, and others.

Pilot Team/Design Team Muddle

One last caution: Some organizations confuse a pilot team with a design team. This mistake is especially common where managers are only testing the self-directed waters instead of making a commitment to teams. Typically, the manager selects several pilot team members from the department and allows them to experiment with changing the process and their roles. If the pilot team is successful, the manager plans to begin new teams.

The problem we have seen with this approach is that the pilot team takes a narrow view of its task, deciding only how *its* team will perform certain tasks. However, what it can do on a small scale is often not possible on a larger one. We know of one pilot team that improved its performance by making all of its work priority jobs so that other, related departments did their jobs before those of the rest of the department. Obviously this strategy would not work on a larger scale.

Similarly, the pilot team members will be able to communicate easily among themselves and may feel no need for a more formalized leadership structure. They often resist making any distinctions among team members. However, were the organization to implement teams across the board, some specialization would probably be required.

The last problem is that the pilot team is often viewed by its peers with a combination of jealousy and anxiety. On the one hand, the pilot team is getting more freedom and support, which generates envy. On the other, employees fear that the pilot team is making decisions on their behalf without their input, which generates fear.

The solution is not to confuse the two roles. Just as the steering committee charters a design team, a design team can charter a pilot group(s) to experiment with innovations. Don't skip the interim step of creating a design team, for you will need its broader focus and representation.

LOW CONFIDENCE

Even with the best guidance and coaching, design team members can have a crisis of confidence. Plucked from a traditional culture where they were expected to check their brains at the door, design team members now find themselves expected to create a better organization, something even their managers seemed incapable of achieving. Fear of failure, skepticism about management's motives, and anxiety about being separated from their flock are all involved.

As we explained in Chapter Three, people evolve through five phases to self-empowerment: denial, testing, participating, responsible, and empowered. The manager will probably not have the luxury of waiting for the design team members to evolve to the highest level before completing the design. They will need varying levels of support from the manager.

Here are some actions managers can take that will increase the design team's confidence:

- Give them training on self-direction and work redesign.
- Educate them about managing change and transition.
- Provide them with relatively easy, less threatening tasks at first (such as establishing group ground rules or analyzing the existing work flow), and celebrate their successes.
- Establish more than one design team at a time. We recommend identifying three teams representing different work areas. Two will tend to compete, but three will tend to share their learning.
- Take the design team members and their co-workers on site visits to other organizations that are further along in the process.
- Provide awareness training to all of the team's co-workers early in the process so that they have an appreciation for and understanding of the design team's tasks.
- At the end of each design team meeting, decide exactly what should be shared with employees and what input is needed. Provide structured yet simple ways for them to carry out this communication. Worksheets, handouts, surveys, formatted flip charts, and the like will all provide them with a crutch to lean on.
- Let team members know that mistakes, problems, and controversy are inevitable. Tell them that every mistake is an opportunity for someone else to take responsibility. This is not an excuse for sloppy

analysis but a recognition of human nature. We often let others take the lead until our dissatisfaction hits a threshold.

• Demonstrate unwavering support for the team's efforts.

CONCLUSION

Most organizations consider themselves as already having "teams." The question they must be careful to ask is: Do we have the right teams? Once macro reorganizational decisions have been made, special attention should be given to the details of how each individual team should be structured and staffed. The best strategy for ensuring good team design is to have a well-prepared and representational committee of line employees and technical experts.

RECOMMENDED READING

Byham, William, and Jeff Cox. *HeroZ: Empower Yourself, Your Coworkers, Your Company*. New York: Harmony Books, 1994.

Hitchcock, Darcy. "Think of Your Design Team as the Lead Raft." *Journal for Quality and Participation* 17 (July–August 1994), pp. 6–10.

Hitchcock, Darcy. *The Work Redesign Team Handbook: A Step-by-Step Guide to Creating Self-directed Teams*. White Plains, NY: Quality Resources, 1994.

Neusch, Donna, and Alan Siebenaler. *The High Performance Enterprise: Reinventing the People Side of Your Business*. Essex Junction, VT: Oliver Wight Publications, 1993.

Chapter Six

Now We Can Do Whatever We Want, Right?

R oles and responsibilities become a major area of confusion for many organizations. Employees hear the term *self-directed* and focus on the word *self*. They quickly grasp some of their new rights without understanding their new responsibilities. Often managers become confused about what they should and shouldn't do. Many step too far back from the team's process, letting them struggle and make mistakes, and then are forced to jump back in. Far too many organizations, particularly the ones that try to implement self-direction on their own or with the aid of a team-building consultant who has no direct experience with self-direction, leave responsibilities vague. *Empowerment* becomes whatever a person wants it to mean.

In this chapter, we examine the common problems of misunderstandings about teams and partnering, confusion about responsibilities, and complications in handing off responsibilities to the team. We provide a structured process for determining team responsibilities and offer a step-by-step process for managers to use when delegating a new responsibility to their teams.

HOW *TEAM* BECOMES A FOUR-LETTER WORD

One of the first problems organizations encounter is a misunderstanding of the word *team*. This word is used to describe a vast array of groups, from departments, project teams, task forces, quality improvement teams, and the like. To confuse matters, many of these groups are not teams at all. Managers have simply applied the term in the hope that it will create a sense of "teamness." This ambiguity can lead to cynicism. The team of the month gets panned on the grapevine. Also, many employees become offended by the insinuation that they have not worked well together in the past. The comment "We've always been a team" is a clear signal that the concept of self-direction is not understood.

Katzenbach and Smith, authors of *The Wisdom of Teams*, provide the following working definition of a generic team:

> A team is a small number of people with complementary skills who are committed to a common purpose, set of performance goals, and approach for which they hold themselves mutually accountable.[1]

Members of many working groups do not possess complementary skills or hold themselves mutually accountable for the results of their groups. However, these attributes are the connective tissue for a self-directed team. In addition, as we explained in Chapter One, a self-directed team is also a natural work group that shares the responsibilities of a traditional supervisor.

Clarifying these distinctions is an important step in everyone's learning process. The following table summarizes some of the main differences between self-directed teams and other teams/groups.

Characteristics	SDWT	Department	Management "Team"	Project Team	Quality Improvement Team	Steering Committee
Natural work group—works together full time	✔	✔		?		
Interdependent—complementary skills needed to complete the task	✔	?	?	✔	✔	?
Jointly accountable for results	✔	?	?	✔	?	?
Shares most or all of responsibilities of traditional supervisor	✔	?				

? = Sometimes　　✔ = Always

---

[1]Jon Katzenbach and Douglas Smith, "The Discipline of Teams," *Harvard Business Review*, April 1993, p. 112.

CONFUSION ABOUT THE NEW
SOCIAL CONTRACT

Managers and employees alike can be confused about their new rights and responsibilities in a self-directed organization.

Misconceptions of Employees

As we have mentioned, many employees interpret self-direction to mean they can do whatever they want, without interference from or concern for their organization, manager, or team. One team at a high-tech manufacturing firm was granted the authority early in its formation of determining the members' own compensation. Not surprisingly, all the members gave themselves handsome raises and nearly bankrupted the department. Clearly they were operating in their own best interests and not in the interests of the company.

Misconceptions of Managers

Some managers suddenly feel powerless, as if they have no rights. In one organization, the team members were verbally abusive to their supervisor, taunting her that her job was at risk. The supervisor felt she had to take the abuse until we explained that she had the same right to be treated with respect that her employees did.

Parents: The Employment McContract

In Chapter One, we introduced the concept of parents versus partners by discussing the different assumptions on which these two management philosophies are based. The manager-as-parent does most of the thinking, sets the rules, and takes care of employees. It is based on a contract of dependence. The manager-as-partner is more egalitarian, sharing the risks, responsibilities, and rewards. It is based on a contract of interdependence.

We have found it immensely helpful to spend time expanding the implications of these two approaches. Clarifying the rights, responsibilities, and results of these two systems with managers and employees goes a long way toward remedying the confusion. A description of the process we use follows. We elicit answers to build a flip chart, a sample of which is shown in Figure 6–1. The remarks in the second and third columns are sample responses supplied by the managers and the employees.

FIGURE 6-1
Parents versus Partners

	Parents	Partners
Assumptions	Employees must be told what to do. They will do as little as possible. They don't know much that would be useful. They are motivated primarily by money and fear.	They have useful knowledge, want to do a good job, are trustworthy, and are motivated primarily by pride, recognition, and accomplishment.
Management rights	Hiring, firing, disciplining, compensating, and goal setting; to decide	Being treated with respect Being involved in decisions that affect them
Management responsibilities	Planning, checking work, telling employees what to do, and taking care of their employees Being accountable for performance Thinking, being right.	Facilitating, coaching, coordinating, sharing information
Employee rights	Quit, fair wages and treatment, safe workplace	Having input into decisions that affect them
Employee responsibilities	Showing up, doing a fair day's work, and doing what they are told	Sharing ideas Being knowledgeable about the big picture Protecting the organization's interests
Boundary setting	Policies, procedures, guidelines Treatment: demotions, promotions, etc.	Values Jointly set policies
Results	Compliance	Commitment

First, we explore the parental paradigm. We ask, "What basic assumptions must managers hold about employees if they are acting as parents?" Typical responses are that employees must be told what to do, they will do as little as possible, they don't know much that would be useful, and they are motivated primarily by money and fear.

Next, we ask, "What are the rights of managers in this environment? What can they do that employees can't?" Hiring, firing, disciplining, compensating, and goal setting are often mentioned. We point out that managers have the right to decide.

Next, we ask, "If managers are to decide, what does the organization expect of them? What are their responsibilities?" Managers are responsible for planning, checking work, telling employees what to do, and taking care of their employees. They are accountable for performance and for keeping the big picture in mind. Since they do the thinking, we expect them to be omniscient and correct.

Then we discuss the rights and responsibilities of employees. Employees have the right to quit; that's better than slavery! They have the right to fair wages, the absence of unlawful discrimination, and a safe workplace. Their responsibilities include showing up, doing a fair day's work, and doing what they are told.

Since every organization needs a way to set boundaries—what is okay and what is not—we explore how this is primarily done in parenting organizations. Official documents such as policies, procedures, and guidelines are mentioned, which, of course, the managers wrote because it is their right to decide. Sometimes unofficial methods are used, such as being demoted, promoted, or transferred and given a challenging assignment.

At best, this system results in compliance. We refer to this system as an "Employment McContract." Like a fast-food burger, you don't ask for much, you don't get much, and little money changes hands. It is a fair arrangement. Employees' rights may be limited, but so are their responsibilities.

Partners: An Addendum to the Contract

Next, we explore the assumptions and responsibilities inherent in the manager-as-partner paradigm. The assumptions about employees are that they have useful knowledge, want to do a good job, are trustworthy, and are motivated primarily by pride, recognition, and accomplishment. The rights of managers change. No longer do they have the sole right to decide. However, they have the right to be treated with respect and to be included in decisions that affect them. Their responsibilities change from doing all the thinking to facilitating, coaching, coordinating, and sharing information.

Employees get both more responsibilities and more rights. Their rights now include having a voice in decisions that affect them. Their responsibilities include—and this is critical for them to understand—making decisions based on the needs of the whole organization. In effect, managers are saying they will share many of their rights, but in return the employees must act in the best interest of the organization.

How the partnering organization establishes boundaries also differs. While not all policies and procedures will disappear, those that remain may be established jointly. The primary basis for establishing boundaries, however, is a shared set of values. Values provide boundaries without the stifling bureaucracy present in most parenting organizations.

This organization results in commitment and dramatically higher performance.

Getting Specific

The distinction between parents and partners seems easy for people to understand, and they readily latch onto the terms. While some may accuse others of wanting to work in a parenting organization, we have never had anyone suggest that they personally did not want to be treated as partners. As usual, however, the devil is in the details. Employees and managers alike are often blind to how they violate these principles.

Both managers and employees need to recognize how their behavior must change to be consistent with the values of partnering. The best way we have found to do this is to give them specific, relevant cases and ask them to consider how a manager or an employee would deal with the situation in both a parenting and a partnering organization. Here are some cases you can use:

- An employee is frustrated about some aspect of work and wants to see it changed.
- The organization is experiencing a significant loss of revenue, which might call for layoffs.
- A manager walks through his department during break and notices that employees are letting the phone ring repeatedly.
- Employees are reluctant to take on handling performance problems within the team and want to continue to pass off these responsibilities to the manager.
- A team is not yet trained on how to hire, but wants to be involved in selecting a new team member.
- One team member just wants to be left alone to do her job. She does excellent work, but does not want to get involved in team meetings or share her knowledge with others.

As you grapple with these issues, make sure people do not vacillate back and forth between parents and partners. This is like a Chinese menu:

Pick combination plate A *or* B; no substitutions. Managers cannot decide that on certain issues they "just have to be the parent sometimes," and' employees cannot periodically avoid the tough issues.

If you are ever stumped about how to proceed, imagine the other party in the situation is an equal partner, a 50-50 owner in a business. How would you handle the situation then? You will find that it is possible to coach someone without being parenting and to admit that you are not yet capable of performing a task without being dependent. No one has yet brought us a situation that could not be handled in a partnering fashion. Challenge your own assumptions until you view the other party as an equal peer.

WHO'S ON FIRST?

Many organizations fail to get specific about the responsibilities the teams should assume. This ambiguity typically leads to several problems: conflict, hoarding of responsibilities, and things dropping through the cracks.

Conflicts

Ambiguity surrounding team responsibilities often results in conflict. Some teams will hold their managers hostage by saying, "We're empowered. We don't need your input." At an auto manufacturer, the teams pushed their managers away when the managers tried to influence a decision by expounding, "That's not team concept!"

Hoarding Responsibilities

Another problem is that some managers may hoard responsibilities. Absent a way to measure the self-directedness of a team, managers often hang onto responsibilities that they enjoy, that they find comfortable, or that they assume the teams could not perform. We were asked to help identify why self-direction had stalled at a chemical plant in Florida. As we talked to front-line employees, we repeatedly heard, "Things haven't changed much; the supervisor still makes most of the decisions." We helped them develop a responsibility list (see Figure 6–2) to clarify how self-directed the teams were expected to become and measure the progress of any team.

Cracks and Costs

The third problem is that important tasks may fall through the cracks. Teams may assume the manager is performing a task, while the manager assumes the opposite.

Other problems are less disruptive, only increasing the costs associated with implementing teams. Without a specific list of responsibilities, it is hard to establish any formalized training. Each manager is forced to do a training needs assessment and spend time coaching each team. These informal coaching sessions are often less reliable than structured, tested training sessions. Also, without the structure a responsibility list provides, it is nearly impossible to establish linkages across teams so that they can support and learn from one another.

Responsibility List

The way to avoid these difficulties is to develop a responsibility list, a detailed listing of tasks the teams should be able to assume over time, as shown in Figure 6–2.

Follow these steps to complete a responsibility list:

1. Add, delete, and modify the tasks on the list until every potential team task is represented and those participating in the process have a shared understanding of what each task means.
2. Identify who performs each task now: management only, technical experts (engineers, human resource directors, etc.), front-line employees, or no one.
3. For any tasks the teams do not now perform, identify those you believe they could eventually assume (focus on the foreseeable future—in two to four years).
4. Code these potential new team tasks:
   - T   Early team responsibility that does not require extensive training or coaching.
   - A   Advanced team responsibility requiring significant training, coaching, or team maturity.
   - S   Shared responsibility with management; both must agree.
   - I   Team should have input, but decision will rest with management.
5. For the T and A tasks, identify whether they should be performed by one individual on the team, a subgroup (as in a hiring committee), or everyone on the team.

6. Cluster the individual and subgroup responsibilities into logical groupings. Clustered tasks for individuals can then be assigned a role name (such as training coordinator, safety star point, etc.). Subgroup tasks imply ad hoc or standing committees the teams may need.

7. Determine selection methods, terms, and performance standards for each role.

FIGURE 6–2
Responsibility List

Task	Does Now	Team Could Do	Code	Responsible
Setting Goals				
Write business plan				
Set team goals				
Set individual goals				
Draft budget				
Approve purchase requests				
Select new equipment/tools				
Managing Work				
Schedule work				
Manage priorities				
Promote safe work practices				
Monitor quality				
Approve time off/vacations				
Schedule time off/vacations				
Monitor attendance				
Staffing Positions				
Assign work on daily basis				
Establish criteria for hiring				
Interview job candidates				

FIGURE 6–2 (continued)
Responsibility List

Task	Does Now	Team Could Do	Code	Responsible
Staffing Positions (cont'd)				
Hire new employees				
Orient new members				
Select team leader				
Decide on promotions				
Terminate employees				
Remove team members				
Conduct Meetings				
Run daily start-up meeting				
Prepare agendas				
Lead problem-solving sessions				
Conduct safety meetings				
Conduct improvement meetings				
Record meeting results				
Coaching Performance				
Establish expectations/standards				
Monitor performance				
Provide informal feedback				
Appraise team members				
Appraise team leaders				
Appraise manager				
Provide on-the-job training				
Define training needs				
Schedule training				
Reinforce training				
Support troubled employees				

FIGURE 6–2 (concluded)
Responsibility List

Task	Does Now	Team Could Do	Code	Responsible
Coaching Performance (cont'd)				
Resolve performance problems				
Offer career guidance				
Communicate upward				
Rewarding Results				
Give verbal praise				
Offer nonmonetary rewards				
Decide on monetary rewards				
Determine pay level of team				
Linking to Others				
Propose ideas to management				
Interact with "customers"				
Interact with "suppliers"				
Coordinate with other departments				
Communicate with management				
Other				

You can also turn the resulting responsibility list into a measurement tool and a training needs assessment.

When discussing the nonteam tasks, *never* say never. Managers and employees are just beginning to understand their capabilities. It is better to say, "We envision that, for the foreseeable future, these other responsibilities will continue to be performed by managers" than to say, "These will always be the responsibility of managers."

PROBLEMS WITH HAND-OFFS

Once managers and employees are clear about the responsibilities the teams can assume, new problems crop up. Many managers struggle with how to stay involved in the decision making. And few are adequately prepared to be effective trainers or coaches.

Coaching from the Sidelines

One of the subtlest and most difficult tasks of the manager is to determine how much to stay involved in the team's decision-making process, how much to let the team struggle, and how far to let the team fail. Some managers err on the side of too much involvement by strongly stating their preferences, hovering over the team, and directing the task. Others err on the side of too little involvement. These managers explain the task and walk away from the field. Then, when the team gets in trouble, the manager rushes from the locker room to save the day. Obviously a balance is needed, but such platitudes do nothing to guide management behaviors.

Coaching Guidelines

Coaching teams is difficult because at any one time, the team's competence and authority vary from one responsibility to the next. It's helpful to place team responsibilities into a matrix that compares competence to authority (see Figure 6–3).

Before taking action, the manager must quickly diagnose the situation by pondering two questions:

- Is this a decision that the team has total authority to decide (within any boundaries given them), or must they get approval?
- Do team members collectively possess all the knowledge necessary to make this decision, or do they lack critical skills or information?

FIGURE 6-3
Coaching Matrix

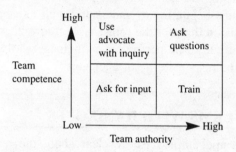

The answers to these questions place the task into one of the quadrants in the matrix.

For responsibilities that fall into the low competence/low authority quadrant, often the best approach is to explain the decision-making process, reasoning, and criteria used to come to a decision. If a decision is in the process of being made, involve the team in critiquing each of these steps along the way. For example, explain the situation as you understand it and ask for input; then explain the proposed decision-making process, and modify it based on their input; then explain the proposed criteria that will guide the choice of options, and solicit their input. This involvement throughout the process will educate them and keep them involved without forcing them to take more responsibility than they are ready to handle.

For decisions that fall into the high competence/low authority quadrant, a technique called "advocate with inquiry" is often the most effective way to help a team. You advocate a position or provide information and then follow up with a question that forces them to consider it. Imagine, for example, that a manager is observing a team struggling with how to improve its process—something it knows quite a lot about. The team, however, does not have total authority to make the changes it wants. Members are discussing an option that the manager knows is impractical. The manager might advocate with inquiry by saying, "Unfortunately, the EPA does not allow us to do that, because it would violate emissions standards. Can you think of any way around this problem?" This technique helps the team to understand where its boundaries lie and why, while still leaving the door open to creative solutions.

For decisions in the high competence/high authority quadrant, it is important that the manager not usurp the team's sense of autonomy. The assumption is that the team possesses all the knowledge and skills necessary to perform the task, even if it does not appear to be are using all of its resources at the moment. If the manager sees the team following a fruitless path, she or he should lead the team with a series of questions. The questions should be designed not to gather data so that the manager can take back the responsibility or express an opinion; instead, the questions should lead the team through an appropriate thought process.

As Larry Miller explains in his book *The American Spirit*,

> The successful manager of the future will make full use of the collective wisdom of those within his jurisdiction and will learn to derive pleasure, not from the making of decisions, but rather from assuring the best possible decision is made.[2]

The questions should reflect this philosophy. Managers must let go of the notion that their job is to find solutions. Instead, their job is now to set in motion a process whereby an enduring solution can be found.

Here is an example set of questions that would be appropriate if a team were solution-jumping: What have you determined the root cause of this problem to be? What alternative solutions might be possible? What risks and potential benefits does each alternative present? What's the worst thing that might happen, and what would you do if it did? Have you considered the impact this might have on other teams?

For decisions in the low competence/high authority quadrant, immediate training and coaching are appropriate. This deserves its own section.

Chalk Talk

To be done correctly, training requires a significant amount of up-front analysis and preparation. Many managers try to "wing it," which leads to inconsistent and unpredictable learning. Since instructional design is a specialized skill, it is often preferable to first send employees to formal training where they can learn the basic skills from an accomplished instructor and a tested program. This should always be supplemented with coaching back on the job.

---

[2]Larry Miller, *American Spirit: Visions of a New Corporate Culture* (New York: William Morrow and Company, 1984).

Where formal training is not an option, it is helpful to get a training specialist to help you plan, design, and evaluate the training. At a minimum, complete the following steps before beginning the training.

First, conduct a "task analysis" that lists all the steps an employee must go through to perform the responsibility correctly. Note anything that is tricky, hard, or critical about performing each step. Also note any helpful tricks of the trade.

Then consider what might prevent employees from performing these tasks. There are three categories of obstacles: skills, motivation, and environment. If the employees do not know how to perform a task, they have a skill deficiency, and training is usually a simple fix. However, people are often sent to training when they know how to do the task but are not motivated to do so or are prevented from doing so by something in the environment (e.g., they don't have the time, they are missing the proper tools).

Resolve any environmental and motivational obstacles before you attempt training. Then negotiate a structured hand-off process with the team. We call our four-step process EARN to emphasize that teams must earn the right to perform these tasks by demonstrating their proficiency.

E Explain the task. Give an overview before going into detail.

A Assist the team while it performs the task. This may entail simulating portions of the task if it is impractical or risky to perform the actual task.

R Review the end product of the team before it goes out.

N Negotiate the team's degree of freedom: Should it recommend, act and report immediately, act and report routinely, or just act?

Imagine, for example, that the team is assuming responsibility for drafting its budget. First, you would explain how the process works, defining unfamiliar terminology and internal conventions. Next you might assist the team in drafting a trial budget and even help it present the budget to the board.

After one or more revision cycles, you may determine that the team is ready for the next step. At the next budgeting cycle, have the team prepare the actual budget and present it to you for review. When members have sufficiently demonstrated—to you and to themselves—that they are ready, you can negotiate the degree of freedom they have around the task. Perhaps you agree that they still pass it by you before submittal, or that they should solicit your input before it is submitted. Or perhaps they can handle the whole process entirely on their own and need not involve you.

This structured EARN process significantly reduces the opportunity for teams to fail. It also imposes a certain discipline on the managers, which not only helps them to slowly recede into the background at a controlled pace but also gives them the time and space to comfortably and confidently let go, thus gradually empowering the team.

CONCLUSION

Perhaps nothing is so important to the successful implementation of self-directed work teams as a clear and common understanding of the principles that define them. Armed with this understanding, organizations are well prepared to make the critical, detailed decisions about how self-direction will work in their particular situation. Without this as a foundation, there is the risk that you will not make the fundamental changes necessary for self-direction to succeed.

RECOMMENDED READING

Belasco, James, and Ralph Stayer. *Flight of the Buffalo: Soaring to Excellence, Learning to Let Employees Lead*. New York: Warner Books, 1993.

Hitchcock, Darcy. "The Key to Understanding Self-Direction. . . Are Your Parents or Partners with Your Employees." *Journal for Quality and Participation,* December 1995, pp. 6–10.

Katzenbach, Jon, and Douglas Smith. *The Wisdom of Teams*. New York: Harper Business, 1993.

Orsburn, Moran, and Zenger Musselwhite. *Self-directed Work Teams: The New American Challenge*. Homewood, IL: Business One Irwin, 1990.

Chapter Seven

We Put You in Teams, So Why Aren't You Working?

M ost organizations vastly underestimate the amount of training and support self-direction requires. These teams do not "just happen" on their own. Choosing self-direction is committing to ongoing development for everyone in the organization. One successful company estimates that each employee spends at least 20 percent of his or her time away from the core job in team-related activities such as training and team meetings.

Within the context of training and support, there are three common reasons self-directed teams fail. Many organizations begin without the proper support roles in place; a champion, an expert in self-direction, and a neutral facilitator are all critical to the success of the team. In addition, organizations typically provide inadequate support to both the manager and the teams. We explore these problems in this chapter.

MISSING CRITICAL ROLES

We have found that three critical support roles must be in place for teams to succeed: a champion, a self-directed guide, and a neutral facilitator. In this section, we explore the problems that occur in their absence, as well as the functions they should perform and the challenges they face.

Champion

What is the role? Regardless of where the initial interest in teams began, you will need a champion, a high-level leader with significant clout who believes passionately in teams. In all of our experience and research, we have yet to encounter an organization that has success-fully launched and maintained self-directed work teams without the strong commitment of top leadership. The absence or loss of a champion with some official authority is one of the most common causes for team collapse.

Who should fill it? This person does not have to hold the title of CEO or president. However, the lower down in the organization you begin, the more limited your success will be. Eventually you will encounter obstacles, such as business systems or other work groups, that will limit your progress.

The champion must be responsible for the area where teams are to be implemented, and that area should be relatively autonomous from other, nonteam portions of the organization. The employees should be predomi-nantly independent from other segments of the organization (except in a customer–supplier relationship), and ideally they should be physically removed from the nonteam employees. Division managers, plant managers, and agency administrators typically have this broad a span of control.

To handle the significant workload associated with implementing teams, some organizations create a full-time champion position that is often filled by a staff person or middle manager of nominal power. This position, which is then removed from line authority, can let managers off the hook. The real champion must have power over the employees being redesigned. A support position can be helpful to perform many of the details, but this person should clearly serve the real champion, not drive the implementation.

What should they do? The champion should perform the fol-lowing tasks:

- Provide a compelling vision.
- Participate in creating a case for change.
- Establish a process through which decisions can be made in the most participative fashion practical (e.g., diagonal-slice steering committees, design teams).
- Advocate for and fund the learning process for all employees.
- Model partnering behaviors and values.
- Protect the teams from naysayers in the early phases.
- Bust barriers as they occur.

- Negotiate expectations with other stakeholders.
- Provide ongoing encouragement and unwavering support.
- Get commitment from those who would replace the champion (when and if the position opens up) that the position will be filled by someone with an equal commitment to teams.

What are their primary challenges?   Champions face several challenges, including a sense of isolation, a barrage of negative reinforcement (naysayers, complainers, jealousies, etc.), and often self-doubt. Jeff Davis, an effective champion and administrator of a progressive county agency in Oregon, offers this advice:

- Be solid and firm in your vision. Don't let anyone shake your resolve.
- Be patient with those around you. They will need lots of time and support to truly integrate this new thinking.
- Be prepared for your own wavering. There will be days you wish you never started this. But there will also be days of great elation and reward.
- Be prepared to commit the necessary time. Davis estimates that in the first year of team implementation, 70 percent of his time was devoted to the effort. He also cautions others not to try to implement a move to self-direction simultaneously with any other significant organizational change.
- Find a trusted mentor who has done it before and with whom you can talk about the emotional expense. Davis emphasizes this point more than all the others. You will fare much better in this process if you acknowledge and share your own personal change with someone who has been there and can empathize and offer advice.

Self-Directed Guide

What is the role?   Those unfamiliar with the failures of teams are condemned to repeat them. If you do not have intimate experience with self-direction, work with someone who does. We have watched far too many organizations make the same common mistakes because, out of either pride or frugality, they insisted on going the path alone. Other organizations hired team-building consultants who lacked specific experience with self-directed teams. Such consultants often miss critical steps.

It does not have to cost a fortune to learn from others' mistakes, and an expert in self-direction can save you many hours and headaches.

Who should fill it?   A self-directed guide should be someone with extensive experience in implementing and supporting self-directed teams. This person need not be on site every hour of every day. However, the guide should be involved throughout the journey.

Here are several relatively inexpensive ways to work with a self-directed guide:

- Attend a workshop that covers the basics about what self-directed work teams are and how to get started. Spend the lunch break with the instructor, and pump him or her for additional information.

- Employ a consultant to help you develop your implementation plan.

- Ask an expert to act as a "shadow consultant," that is, meet privately with the champion to help direct the effort.

- Hire a consultant to sit in on your steering committee meetings, at least once a month.

- Fill open management positions with people who have implemented teams and worked inside a self-directed organization.

- Develop a network and meet regularly with others outside your organization who are implementing teams so that you can support one another.

Don't be penny wise and pound foolish.

What should the guide do?   The self-directed guide can perform some or all of the following functions, but keep in mind that you should always do as much as you can in-house:

- Provide a structured process for planning the implementation and help the organization fill in the details.

- Design and conduct awareness training.

- Provide a structured team launch process, including required training.

- Provide a process for assessing the readiness of the organization.

- Get the steering committee and/or design teams off to a good start and then support them as needed.

- Provide a structure for conducting training needs assessments.
- Arrange site visits at other organizations or refer you to others who are implementing teams.
- Inform you of educational opportunities such as conferences, public workshops, books, articles, and the like.
- Educate, train, and coach managers and facilitators.
- Confront inconsistent behavior when others will not (e.g., with executives).
- Be a coach to the champion and the champion's manager.
- Provide proactive/preventative guidance and ad hoc consulting.
- Intervene with troubled teams.
- Provide advice about how to change organizational systems.

What are the guide's primary challenges?   The person who fills this role can come from either inside or outside the organization. Each has its benefits and drawbacks. Internal consultants have the advantage of understanding the culture and power relationships. The drawbacks are that the consultant may be in a subordinate position to those needing to be coached and may lack the breadth of experience and contacts an external consultant might have.

For an external consultant, the situation is reversed. In addition, we sometimes find clients are reluctant to use external consultants long enough to get the full benefit of their knowledge. To some, consultants are like circling sharks, something to keep *at least* at arm's length. If a client does not let us become a partner in its process, it limits the benefits we can bring. If the facilitators and champion have significant experience with self-direction, this arm's-length relationship is not usually a problem as long as someone is ensuring consistency of models, approaches, and terms. However, some of the tasks mentioned above, such as confronting inappropriate behavior and providing proactive guidance, are difficult or impossible without a close, ongoing relationship.

Facilitator

What is the role?   The term *facilitator* is used to describe many different roles, including a meeting facilitator, an empowering manager, and an internal consultant acting as a disinterested third party. We are referring here to internal consultants who are trained in team building and group process. Teams and their managers benefit from the observations of a neutral outsider. Without this view, teams typically miss significant opportunities to improve, and when teams and their managers butt heads, there is no one to facilitate a resolution.

Who should fill it? Organizations have taken different approaches to filling facilitator positions. Some have rotated managers through the position. This approach provides managers with critical developmental opportunities and may make it easier for them to confront other managers. The potential downside is that managers are often viewed by employees as a clique, and this belief will inhibit open and honest communication. If you take this approach, be careful to initially select managers who are respected and trusted by the front line.

Other organizations select front-line employees to be facilitators. These individuals may have the trust of their peers, but may lack the impact when forced to confront management. If you follow this approach, select individuals who are respected informal leaders and have excellent communication skills.

What should the facilitator do? The facilitator should do as little as necessary to help the team and its manager. For instance, she or he may have to facilitate some of the early team meetings, but should quickly work out of that role. Facilitators typically perform these functions:

- Facilitate team meetings.
- Sit in on meetings and provide process observations.
- Consult with the star points and managers.
- Conduct team-building activities.
- Assist the team in selecting and administering appropriate assessments.
- Share learning across teams.
- Bring undiscussables to the surface.
- Conduct training sessions.
- Report to the steering committee.
- Secure additional resources for the team.
- Mediate disputes within and across teams.
- Encourage teams and team members to take responsibility.
- Facilitate design team meetings.

What are the facilitator's primary challenges? Facilitators struggle with several problems: overshadowing the manager, inadequate training and support, and being viewed as a member of an elite clique. Facilitators must be careful not to strip authority or responsibility from the team's managers. Many managers feel uncertain enough about their viability and purpose. Having a facilitator step in and take over the coaching of the team only increases their confusion and feelings of impotence. Instead, the facilitator should view his or her role as standing behind the manager—not doing for the manager, but helping the manager to do.

Coupled with this problem is managers who abdicate to the facilitators. At Microsoft Manufacturing and Distribution, one facilitator reported that when he showed up to observe a team meeting, the supervisor turned the meeting over to him and left to do his "real job." A similar situation arose at the Oregon Department of Transportation. Early in its team implementation, the department identified and trained 70 full- and part-time facilitators to support its 600 teams all across the state. While the facilitators received thorough skill training, they still fell into the trap of assuming too much responsibility for the teams. They began to take on all kinds of team and leadership roles. The result was a level of codependency that was crippling the teams and disabling the managers. Facilitators should avoid enabling managers. Implementing teams is the manager's responsibility; the facilitator is there only as a trained observer and coach.

Facilitators are often the messengers of what is viewed as bad news. In this role, they can catch a significant amount of abuse. Certainly they need thorough training on group process skills. But in addition, they require the ongoing support of management and a self-directed coach. They inevitably will encounter problems they cannot solve, such as an intractable supervisor. They need a close and supportive relationship with the champion and other managers to step in when needed. They also need someone from whom to get advice when the situation seems to exceed their current training or ability.

Because of their tough role, facilitators tend to stick together. They may discuss problems and potential solutions. If they are not careful, they can be perceived as violating confidences and as becoming a clique. Since we believe they will need one another's support, it is better to continue sharing information. However, facilitators should present a united front and be introduced as a team whose members are *expected* to share information among themselves.

The Oregon Department of Transportation used this approach to regroup and reform its facilitators in response to its codependency and other problems. It hired 10 full-time internal consultants with significant organization development experience and then selected 25 agency employees to fill "rotational" facilitator positions. The 10 specialists support the rotational positions, which in turn serve as local resources, coaching and consulting with the teams in their areas. The plan is to phase out the 25 rotational positions over the next two to four years once the teams are operating self-sufficiently. To ensure consistency in their approach and continue their own development, these 35 consultants and facilitators convene in some regional team several times a year to add to their tool kits, give feedback to one another, network, and renew their vision.

INADEQUATE SUPPORT FOR MANAGERS

Managers are pivotal in the change to self-direction, but they also bear a double burden. They must simultaneously withstand their own transition while helping the teams weather theirs. Some have described the experience as akin to presiding over their own funerals.

To make matters worse, managers in traditional organizations are guarded about their own development. They are used to getting the executive overview of any training rather than sitting through it in its entirety themselves. Also, as a group they are somewhat reluctant to reveal their own weaknesses and vulnerabilities. Put all this together and you get a recipe for disaster. Managers grossly underestimate the support they will need, and since they are usually the ones planning the implementation, getting them to accept more is a challenge.

The self-directed guide can help establish realistic expectations and the champion should model learning. Keep the following pitfalls in mind.

Leading with Skills

Through their research, Beer and Eisenstat of Harvard Business School and Spector of Northeastern University concluded that most change efforts were based on a flawed theory of change:

> The common belief is that the place to begin is the knowledge and attitudes of individuals. Changes in attitudes, the theory goes, lead to changes in individ-

ual behavior . . . This theory gets the change process exactly backward . . . The most effective way to change behavior, therefore, is to put people into a new organizational context, which imposes new roles, responsibilities, and relationships on them . . . it forces new attitudes and behaviors on people.[1]

This is consistent with our research and experience. We also believe it is particularly true for managers and executives. For example, in *The Lessons of Experience: How Successful Executives Develop on the Job*, authors McCall, Lombardo, and Morrison discovered in numerous interviews with successful executives that training was *never* mentioned as a significant factor in their development. Training had served mostly as an ego boost. The managers were honored to be sent to a prestigious program or were surprised to discover they knew as much as or more than other respected managers.[2]

Managers change when their environment changes. Early interventions with managers should be focused not on providing skills but on exposing them to information about how their environment is changing.

In 1994, Axis Performance Advisors conducted a survey to discover what strategies were found to be most effective in helping managers make the transition. The most effective methods involved the managers in creating their own new roles. The top three methods were

- Taking them on site visits on which they could talk with peers in more advanced organizations.
- Involving them in the redesign of the workplace.
- Giving them access to a consultant on demand.

It seems that until they have internalized the need for change and their new roles, managers are covered with Teflon; training won't stick.

Presenting data about the work environment was also helpful. Climate surveys, team assessments, and information from team members filtered through a third party were all considered better than average as a change strategy. The results of our survey are summarized in the appendix to this chapter.

---

[1]Dale Tompkins, "Creating the Context for Change," white paper, Ernst and Young.

[2]Morgan McCall, Michael Lombardo, and Ann Morrison, *The Lessons of Experience: How Successful Executives Develop on the Job* (Lexington, MA: Lexington Books, 1988).

Using Low-Impact Strategies

In our study, we also found that the frequency with which each strategy was used had no correlation to its effectiveness. Some of the most useful methods were rarely used. For example, providing access to a consultant on demand (designated on the charts as "consulting") was used by fewer than 25 percent of the organizations. Some of the less effective methods, however, were used a lot. For example, informal sharing among managers was used most frequently, yet it scored in the middle of the pack on effectiveness. Passive methods such as reading and videos were also used more often than their effectiveness might justify.

Focusing on Training Instead of Development

The implementation is expensive enough without wasting money on low-impact methods. One common error is to view the issue as training rather than development. Training emphasizes formal workshops and seminars. While these are an important component, they are in no way sufficient. Instead, you should view learning as primarily a matter of orchestrating a series of experiences that lead the managers through their own personal transition.

This must include private coaching, personal assessments, and observation. Managers need help translating course concepts into their everyday work so that supporting teams is not something extra but an integral part of how they do their jobs. They must learn how to demonstrate their commitment through their actions, not their words. They must also learn how to use every interaction and staff meeting as a way to further the team's growth. This does not happen in the artificial setting of a workshop.

Turning up the Heat

We find it helpful to plan these experiences over time, providing feedback on a scale from nonthreatening to quite direct. We have laid out some of the options on a thermometer to show their relative perspiration factor (see Figure 7–1).

Over time, you should plan experiences that slowly turn up the heat on managers to change. Obviously, reassignment or termination should be a last resort, used only after it is clear that the manager cannot or will not adapt to a partnering style.

FIGURE 7–1
Strategies for Encouraging Change

- Reassign or terminate.
- Develop a performance plan.
- Tie team results and performance to managers' rewards.
- Include coaching in performance appraisals and measures.
- Conduct upward appraisals.
- Explicitly model desired behaviors.
- Provide on-the-job coaching.
- Provide specific tasks for managers to perform after training.
- Observe the manager in action and model unobtrusively.
- Facilitate meetings where managers can discuss their challenges.
- Provide skills training.
- Take managers on site visits.
- Send managers to conferences, professional association meetings, and so on.
- Expose managers to information through reading, briefings, tapes, and the like.

How to Deal with People Who "Don't Get It"

A team-based organization is not for everyone. Organizations often treat those who can't adapt as if they are intractable and uncooperative. They tend to revert to parental behaviors: cajoling, chastising, punishing. Remember, however, we said that a fundamental belief in partnering is that people want to do a good job.

Imagine that you computerized an administrative process that now requires that employees have far better eyesight. Let's say you have a nearsighted employee who can no longer do her work, and no modification of the equipment is possible. What would you do with her? Certainly you wouldn't tell her she has to get on board, or else. You wouldn't say she's old-fashioned. You'd acknowledge that the nature of her work has changed and try to find a more appropriate position for her. If another employee was inhibited by poor typing skills, you'd give him training. And if he decided that he didn't like working with computers, you'd try to find a position that better matched his interests.

You should treat anyone who can't adapt to teams with the same dignity and respect. It is not fair to demean people for being well indoctrinated into our individualistic culture. As equal partners, examine the current organizational realities and help these individuals find places where their attributes will be assets.

INADEQUATE SUPPORT FOR TEAMS

"The worst thing you can do to a team is to leave it alone in the dark. I guarantee that if you come across someone who says teams didn't work in his company, it's because management didn't take an interest in them."[3] So says James Watson, vice president of Texas Instruments. Teams need ongoing support throughout their transition. Far too many organizations think they can send their team to a one-day workshop and *violà*, an instant team is formed. One client, a steel manufacturer, hired us several years ago to provide its team with a two-day training session and then suspended formal training. To this date, the client is still struggling, having missed most of the potential benefits self-direction could have brought. The survival of its entire venture is in question because of its shortsightedness.

We see the training process as a series of steps with an underlayment of corresponding management development (see Figure 7–2).

Before the teams begin operation, they should complete both some preparatory training and a team launch process. The preparatory training should include

- An introduction to high-performance and quality principles and the organization's case for change.
- Familiarity with what self-directed work teams are and how they function.
- A grounding in team-building fundamentals.
- Honing of their interpersonal and conflict resolution skills.

The team launch process represents steps teams should perform to get ready to work together. They should complete

---

[3]Brian Dumaine, "Who Needs a Boss?", *Fortune*, May 7, 1990, p. 58.

FIGURE 7-2
The Team Development Process

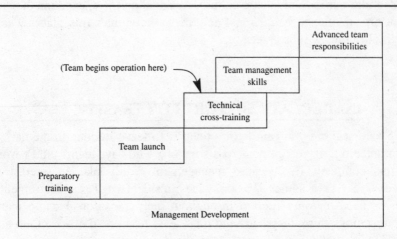

- A clearly articulated set of team agreements (sometimes called *ground rules*) and defined leadership roles.
- A customer survey process to define a set of critical customer requirements.
- A charter that describes the team's mission and key result areas.
- A process diagram that shows how the team will perform its primary functions.
- A set of performance measures and a system for tracking progress.
- An established meeting process and templates for outcome-based agendas.
- A process for acknowledging achievements.

The technical cross-training on job functions should begin shortly before the team is expected to begin operation and may continue indefinitely, depending on the degree of cross-training required. Any leadership responsibilities not requiring training can also be delegated at this time.

Once the team is technically proficient in its tasks, early leadership responsibilities can be handed off, one by one. The team management training is based on the responsibility list (refer to Chapter Six).

Once the team has assumed all early team responsibilities, the advanced hand-offs can begin.

CONCLUSION

Many organizations heave a big sigh of satisfaction once they have teams up and running. While this milestone is cause for celebration, it doesn't mean the job is done. Without adequate support staff (champion, guide, facilitator) and sufficient resources (training and pressure strategies), teams can wither from lack of attention. To the extent that you can, plan ahead and have these resources in place. You will greatly increase the likelihood that your efforts will maintain momentum.

RECOMMENDED READING

Fisher, Kimball. *Leading Self-Directed Work Teams*. New York: McGraw-Hill, 1993.

Fisher, Kimball, Steven Rayner, and William Belgard. *Tips for Teams*. New York: McGraw-Hill, 1995.

Geber, Beverly. "From Manager into Coach," *Training*, February 1992, pp. 25–31.

Gordon, Jack. "The Team Troubles That Won't Go Way." *Training*, August 1994, pp. 25–34.

Larson, Carl E., and Frank M. J. LaFasto. *Teamwork: What Must Go Right/What Can Go Wrong*. Newbury Park, CA: Sage Publications, 1989.

Rees, Fran. *How to Lead Work Teams: Facilitation Skills*. San Diego: Pfeiffer & Co., 1991.

Willard, Marsha. "Turning Up the Heat." *Journal for Quality and Participation*, July–August 1995.

Appendix
Helping managers change

Final Results of the Change Strategies Survey

In 1994, Axis Performance Advisors conducted a survey to determine the most effective methods for helping managers transform from a traditional style to empowering leadership. This survey measured the effectiveness and use of a variety of methods. Approximately 100 organizations were surveyed from all sectors: manufacturing, health care, government, nonprofit, utilities, and other. Respondents were asked to check all the methods they had used and then rate each method on its effectiveness on a scale of 1 to 5, with 5 being "very effective." This appendix summarizes our findings. We have analyzed the effectiveness and use of methods for three populations: all respondents, those who rated their organizations as empowered (from participative management to organizational democracy), and those who rated their organizations as low in empowerment (traditional management to quality circles). A legend of methods is listed at the end.

The primary finding is that no correlation exists between effectiveness and use. In general, organizations preferred low-cost methods that carried little accountability for change. Alternatively, the most effective methods were often those that were potentially uncomfortable and carried an expectation of change. Bear in mind that some items had high standard deviations, indicating that respondents differed significantly in how effective they found a particular method.

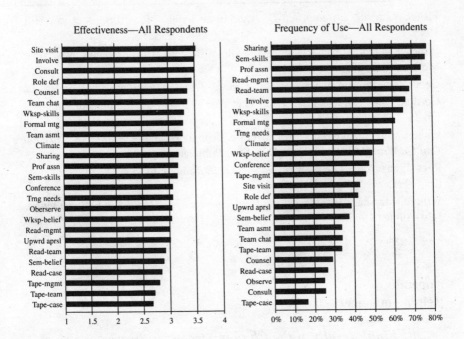

Results for Empowered Organizations

Interesting differences show up when you look only at the respondents who rated their organizations high on the empowerment scale (including participative management, self-directed, and organizational democracy). Usage of the various methods did not change much. However, the effectiveness of all the methods improved, and giving managers access to consultants on demand was rated at the top, the only item that averaged 4 on a 5-point scale. The top 10 in effectiveness included all of the same items in slightly different positions, with one notable exception: Having a consultant observe and give a manager feedback moved up to fourth in effectiveness; it had been 16th on the other chart. It seems that being open to feedback may be a critical component in creating change in the culture.

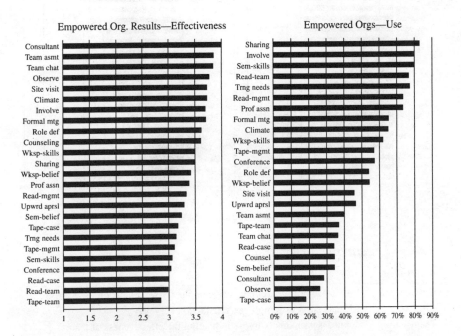

Results for Traditional Organizations

Those who rated their organizations low in empowerment primarily used methods that carry little accountability and cost. Reading, training, informal sharing, professional association meetings, and conferences were popular. Overall, all methods were viewed as less effective compared to the more empowered organizations. This may be due to respondents not having been in the process long enough to see the results or due to intractable managers. Some of the same practices were at the top of their lists such as those involving consultants and site visits. One important difference is that conferences were rated first in effectiveness, whereas they were near the bottom of the list for empowered organizations.

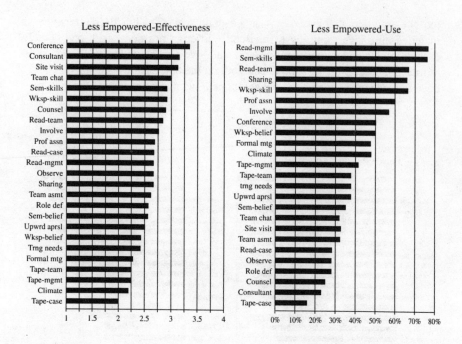

Less Empowered-Effectiveness

Less Empowered-Use

Legend of Survey Items

Assessments

Upwrd aprsl	Upward appraisals (employees complete assessments on their boss)
Climate	Climate surveys (employee satisfaction surveys)
Team asmt	Team assessments (surveys indicating the effectiveness of teams)

Training

Wksp-skills	In-house workshops on management skills (coaching, leadership, etc.)
Sem-skills	Public seminars on management skills (coaching, leadership, etc.)
Wksp-belief	In-house workshops on management beliefs/philosophy
Sem-belief	Public seminars on management beliefs/philosophy
Conference	Conferences on self-direction or management

Involvement

Involve	Involving managers/supervisors in directing the redesign effort
Role def	Involving managers/supervisors in defining their future role
Trng needs	Involving managers/supervisors in identifying their own training needs

Networking

Formal mtg	Conducting formal meetings among managers to share challenges
Sharing	Encouraging informal sharing of information between managers/supervisors
Site visit	Taking managers on site visits to meet with peers in other organizations
Prof assn	Attending professional association meetings

Coaching/Mentoring ("consultant" may be internal or external expert)

Counsel	Providing managers with private counseling sessions with "consultant"
Observe	Having "consultant" observe manager and provide feedback
Consultant	Provide access on demand to "consultant" as requested by manager
Team chat	Having "consultant" chat with team members to monitor progress

References and Resources

Read-team	Books/articles on self-direction and empowerment
Read-mgmt	Books/articles on leadership and management
Read-case	Books/articles on case studies
Tape-team	Videos/films on self-direction and empowerment
Tape-mgmt	Videos/films on leadership and management
Tape-case	Videos/films on case studies

III

KNOCKING DOWN
HURDLES

O nce teams are up and running, there is still much to do. Organizational systems must be redesigned to accommodate teamwork
instead of individual work. Certain legal concerns must be addressed. To
get the most from self-direction, the organization must be able to share its
learning across boundaries. Perhaps most critical, the organization must
be prepared to withstand organizational crises while remaining true to the
principles of self-direction.

In Chapter Eight, "Who Sets Goals and Measures?," we cover the
planning and tracking of performance. Traditional management-by-objectives planning systems are inappropriate for teams. Furthermore, the measures an organization needs to promote quality and teamwork are quite
different from traditional measures. In Chapter Eight, we provide guidelines for designing team-based goal setting and measurement systems
that optimize the performance of the organization. We also provide a
worksheet for creating a balanced set of measures.

In Chapter Nine, "How Do We Appraise and Reward Performance?,"
we address how traditional appraisal and compensation systems interfere
with team functioning. Both are based on inappropriate assumptions that
must be openly acknowledged and refuted before appropriate systems can
be invented. Frankly, few organizations have crossed the starting line to

the radical changes ahead. In this chapter, we provide leading-edge guidelines for redesigning feedback and compensation systems to support self-direction.

In Chapter Ten, "Close Encounters with the Law," we address legal concerns associated with self-directed teams. What happens when teams begin to invade territories governed by union contracts, civil service regulations, and labor law? While loosely interpreted legal language leaves open the risk of legal action, this chapter suggests several strategies for steering a course around the legal land mines.

In Chapter Eleven, "The Immune Response," we deal with an organization's desperate drive to maintain the status quo. Organizations often ignore the reasons for their own success, preferring to attribute results to less threatening causes than self-direction. This chapter explores appropriate responses to individuals, departments, or situations that effectively hold successful teams in check.

Even when you've done everything by the book, your efforts can still be derailed by events out of your control. In Chapter 12, "Bait 'n Switch," we explore two of the most common problem-causing situations: change in leadership and economic reversals. Though we can't promise they will never happen, we offer suggestions for how to best weather them. Since few organizations seldom do enough to inoculate themselves against these situations, our recommendations range from conservative to the speculative.

After reading Part III, you will understand the primary systemic issues that must be addressed for teams to succeed over the long term. Then, in the last chapter, we ask you to explore with us what we believe is the next step after self-direction: organizational democracy.

Chapter Eight

Who Sets Goals and Measures?

S elf-directed teams require changes in most organizational systems. Often the first set of systems that act as barriers to the teams is the performance management process. This includes setting goals, establishing measures, monitoring and appraising performance, and rewarding people. For the vast majority of organizations, these systems still reflect a parenting paradigm: Managers must tell employees what to do and build in controls and bribes to make sure they perform.

In this chapter, we address the first two systems in the process that represent the planning phase: setting goals and measures. Appraisals and rewards, which tend to be largely after-the-fact steps, are covered in the next chapter.

Goals and their associated measures suffer from two common problems that affect the performance of self-directed teams. First, if goals are broken down to an actionable level, they are usually focused on individual performance rather than on teams. Second, goals are established by management and are often viewed as arbitrary rather than strategic. In this chapter, we discuss each of these common problems and explain how to design an effective, team-oriented goal-setting process. We also describe the types of measures teams should track and provide a worksheet to help you define a comprehensive set of team measures for your own organization.

FOCUSING ON THE WRONG THING

Traditionally managers have been taught to focus on individual performance. Professors of Supervision 101 state that a task should never be delegated to more than one individual. How else can you hold someone accountable for his or her performance? Unfortunately, this fixation on individual performance often results in poor teamwork.

Why Individual Goals and Measures Lead to Suboptimization

Conventional wisdom maintains that setting individual goals improves performance. Imagine that you managed four self-directed teams, each team performing the same interdependent task. In one team, you gave each team member an individual goal. In the second team, you only set a goal for the team as a whole. The third team was given both individual and team goals. The fourth team was given no specific goal at all. Which team would perform the worst?

Most people would say the team with no goals would perform the worst. And they would be wrong. In a study that replicated this situation, the team with *individual* goals performed the worst of all four groups— worse, in fact, than the team with no goal at all! The team with both individual and team goals performed the best, but the difference in its performance was not statistically significant compared to the no-goal and team-goal conditions.[1]

What should we learn from this study? Where employees are interdependent (one of the key characteristics of a team), focusing on individual performance is a mistake. It encourages people to compete with one another, which suboptimizes the performance of the group. The absence of a clear and collaboratively crafted team goal also makes mutual accountability unachievable.

Most organizations would claim they have both individual and team goals. Technically they would be correct, but from a psychological perspective they would be wrong. Where employees are given individual performance goals, measured against those goals, and paid at least in part based on achievement of those goals, the individual goals overshadow the group goals. Even in organizations that offer gain sharing or profit sharing, this overshadowing is barely mitigated. Since the "line of sight"—the personal sense of control over performance—lessens as you focus on larger and larger groups, employees are still more likely to focus on indi-

---

[1]T. Mitchell and W. Silver, "Individual and Group Goals When Workers Are Interdependent: Effects on Task, Strategies and Performance," *Journal of Applied Psychology* 75, no. 2 (1990), pp. 185–93.

vidual instead of group performance unless extraordinary care is exercised to keep them focused on the overarching goals.

Picking the Right Group

Once the importance of focusing on team goals is recognized, the next question is "Which team?" For you can create the same suboptimization if measures and goals are focused on too small a group. For example, most manufacturing operations measure performance by shift. This leads to competition among shifts. At a high-tech manufacturing plant, one shift complained that the previous shift frequently ignored maintenance procedures in its attempt to produce the most product. The following shift came on assuming critical components had been replaced on the equipment, only to find itself quickly turning out substandard product. Focusing on individual shifts, work cells, or teams encourages employees to cut corners and creates problems for those in other groups.

The other extreme, setting overall goals for the organization only, is often equally unworkable. No one would have any direction. The solution is to have goals at all levels, but focus attention on the "primary functional unit" of the organization.

The primary functional unit (PFU) is the level at which the group is relatively autonomous from other groups. At this level, the work process is largely independent from that of other groups, and competition from other groups would not significantly affect the group's performance or learning.

Most organizations can be viewed as concentric rings, with the individual at the center (see Figure 8–1). Ask yourself: At what level is our work largely autonomous from that of the other groups? In most cases, the answer is at the division level.

Identifying this primary functional unit is a judgment call. For example, Monsanto's Pensacola plant divided their 2,000-plus employees into three product groups and divided each product group into smaller teams. Initially it focused on these smaller teams but found the groups competing to the detriment of performance. Now it views the entire site as its PFU. We suspect it will ultimately determine that the product groups represent the optimal level.

Goals, measures, and compensation should be concentrated at the PFU. These goals and measures can bear consequences because the group is large enough that collectively it represents most of the system that

FIGURE 8-1
Finding the Primary Functional Unit

affects performance. All groups below this primary functional unit should be focused on how they contribute to the PFU.

Psychologically, the goals and measures for the PFU should over-shadow all others. Creating this preeminence depends on taking certain actions and avoiding others. Each team should participate in the PFU planning process and report on how it is contributing to the unit's results. The unit's performance against goals and measures should be reported regularly to all employees. Those within the primary functional unit should be held jointly accountable for its performance (such as having a portion of compensation dependent on its performance), and a mecha-nism for coordinating activities should be in place.

Below the primary functional unit, goals and measures should be used only for learning. Teams should not be played off one another. If one team seems to be outperforming another, this should be an opportunity for exploration, not one-upsmanship.

The plant manager of a manufacturing company made a tactical mis-take when faced with this situation. Of four shifts, team A had dramati-cally higher performance. He asked team A to train the other shifts. Pre-dictably, this created hostility among them. Through his actions, the plant manager drew too much attention to the team measures. In addition, he may have been rewarding a team that was circumventing proper procedures, leaving messes for the next shift.

Instead, he should have set up a mechanism allowing the teams to regularly share ideas, techniques, and innovations in a cooperative environment. If the plant manager mentioned the team results at all, his comments should have had the tone of curiosity instead of judgment. "I thought it was interesting that team A's measures have been higher than the other teams'; do you have any idea what might be causing that?" is preferable to "team A did better than you; find out why."

Edgar Schein, author of *Leadership and Organizational Culture*, identified five primary mechanisms leaders have to influence the culture of the organization. The first is "what leaders pay attention to, measure, and control."[2] Managers must be careful to pay most attention to the results of the primary functional unit, not the results of individual teams.

How to Address Individual Performance Issues

Along these same lines, managers must treat individual performance as a private matter for the team. On a team, individual contributions vary. As long as the team is satisfied with individual contributions and the overall performance of the team is adequate, you should not get involved in assessing individual goals or measures. Certainly, if the team believes it cannot resolve a performance problem, you should help: But otherwise, stay out. Treat it as you would the behavior of a married couple: It's none of your business unless they ask for help or unless the behavior is directly affecting you.

Years ago, one of us managed a team of instructional designers. One member of this team did not perform at the same level as the others if you measured performance by the number of pages of training manuals produced. However, everyone on the team believed his or her insights and humor were ample compensation. No one ever complained about his or her performance. Other teams have been known to carry members during personal crises, an act that only strengthens their bond. You need to grant your teams the freedom to define adequate individual performance.

---

[2]Edgar Schein, *Leadership and Organizational Culture: A Dynamic View* (San Francisco: Jossey Bass). The other four factors are leader reactions to critical incidents and organizational crises; deliberate role modeling; criteria for allocation of rewards and status; and criteria for recruitment, selection, promotion, retirement, and excommunication.

WHAT'S WRONG WITH MBO

Management by objectives (MBO) has been an honored process in most organizations for many years. However, this approach to planning is inappropriate in a self-directed environment.

Top-Down Goal Setting as a Parenting Task

Most planning and measurement systems are top-down. Executives set strategy, division managers write operational plans to meet the strategic plan, middle managers write departmental plans to meet the operational plans, and so on. While this management-by-objectives process makes sense, it reflects the manager-knows-best parental perspective. It is not empowering to be told what you must do and be left to figure out how to do it. Also, it is unwise for executives to ignore the front-line knowledge of changing customer needs. The arrogance of claiming to know what the customer wants without firsthand knowledge has crippled such giants as General Motors and IBM. You must find a way to integrate the executives' long-term view with the practical insights of those on the front line.

Arbitrary Targets Turn Off Employees

Another common problem with the top-down approach is that the goals often seem arbitrary: Increase production by 15 percent; reduce your budget by 10 percent; serve 25 percent more customers. This trend toward arbitrariness has actually increased with the popularity of six-sigma concepts that encourage organizations to seek extremely small defect rates, whether or not those goals are feasible.

Such goals must be grounded in customer and competitive needs, and there must be some reason to believe the goals are possible to achieve. For example, Motorola set a goal of 3.4 defects per million.[3] This goal was ambitious, but it was based on knowledge about the performance of their Japanese competitors. Without this, such goals seem manipulative to employees, making them feel as if they are being asked only to work harder, not smarter.

---

[3]Mark G. Brown, Darcy Hitchcock, and Marsha Willard, *Why TQM Fails and What to Do About It* (Burr Ridge, IL: Irwin Professional Publishing, 1994), p. 12.

GOAL SETTING AS A SINE WAVE

Instead of being a unidirectional process, setting strategy and goals should oscillate like a sine wave among all levels of the organization (see Figure 8–2). In small organizations, it may be possible to bring everyone together into a future search conference or a similar whole-systems conference model. In larger organizations, you may be able to use a representative process. Whether the process is performed with all stakeholders in the room or is done in stages, the following steps should be included:

FIGURE 8–2
Planning as a Sine Wave

Executives

| Front-line briefing | Strategy setting | Operational planning/ budgeting | Final adjustments to plan |

Front-line employees

1. Executives should be briefed firsthand by those on the front lines. This is best done through the use of targeted questions to those with direct customer and competitor contact: What factors seem to be the most important in creating repeat business? For the customers we have lost (or who are not using us exclusively), what are their reasons for using our competitors? Related to our products and services, what do our customers struggle with the most, and what products or services might we invent that would thrill them? In large corporations, technologies such as E-mail and teleconferences can be used to gather these data efficiently. Executives can ask similar questions of key customers as well.

2. This new knowledge should be evaluated against the organization's strategy. Some issues may be of no consequence since they relate to niches the organization does not intend to serve. However, some issues may reveal changing customer needs and expectations that imply a need to change strategies or develop entirely new products and services.

3. The new strategy should then be communicated and explained to all employees. Providing a brochure of the strategic goals is inadequate. Employees must have an opportunity to ask questions about the ramifications of those goals and the strategic issues the goals are intended to

address. This process should be a dialogue, not simply a formal presentation. All employees should be clear about the impact the strategic plan will have on their PFU.

4. Finally, the business plans for the PFUs should begin at the front lines and be rolled up from the bottom of the organization, not down from the top.

At a division of an auto manufacturer where we implemented such a process, managers were initially resistant to this approach. They feared their employees would only ask for "gimmes," frivolous, self-centered bobbles that the managers would then have to turn down. In addition, some of their front-line employees lacked a high school education, and some could not even read, so many managers doubted their ability to handle such an important task. They were truly amazed at the quality of ideas that were generated by asking employees to participate in the formal business planning process.

Many teams asked for small items that would help them perform better, such as walkie-talkies to communicate across millions of square feet of plant floor. Others became excited about becoming profit centers and offering services to groups outside the corporation. One group of UAW union employees that operated a small power plant on site built a five-year plan to shut the plant down and redeploy themselves. The moral? Do not underestimate your employees.

These team plans and associated budgets should then be rolled up through the organization, balancing the ideas with the strategic needs of the PFU and the larger organization. Where changes are deemed necessary, the team should receive feedback and be permitted to adjust its goals.

We have found this process yields far more in creative ideas, tangible improvements, and employee commitment than any traditional planning process we have seen.

DEFINING MEASURES

Tom Malone of Milliken and Company says, "Teams that don't keep score are only practicing."[4] However, as we discussed earlier, not just any measurement will do. Several issues must be addressed.

---

[4]Steven M. Hronec, *Vital Signs: Using Quality, Time, and Cost Performance Measurements to Chart Your Company's Future* (New York: AMACOM, 1993), p. 14.

Linking Measures to Mission and Strategy

To be useful, any measurement system should link directly to the organization's mission and strategy. If you intend to be the airline of choice for business travelers, you should have a way of knowing how well you are doing with business travelers. If you intend to be the lowest-cost provider of corrugated boxes or electricity, you should have a way to measure your costs relative to the competition. If you need to be the employer of choice for nurses within your geographic territory, your measures should indicate whether you are your applicants' first choice.

The measurement system must be tailored to the organization. Examine your mission and business plan and ask, "How will we know how well we are doing?" This will help you measure what is important, not just what is easy to measure.

How Many Measures Are Enough?

Many organizations measure "administrivia." Far too many customer service representatives are measured on the average length of calls instead of on the quality of service they provide. Ongoing measures should track the vital few, not the trivial many. A team can always institute temporary measures to identify and solve specific problems, but these measures shouldn't be elevated to permanent status unless they are truly critical. Each person or team should have to focus on only a handful of measures on a regular basis.

ADC Kentrox Corporation, a division of ADC that manufactures telecommunications equipment, provides a good example. The company measures and reports to workers on a quarterly basis what it calls its "Six Ups." These are six key measures of profitability and customer service:

- Customer request versus ship date.
- Customer returns versus sales.
- First contact to resolve customer issues.
- Revenue growth over prior period.
- Return on sales.
- New-product revenues as a percentage of total.

These six measures keep the company focused on what it has determined to be its few critical success factors. Every team or unit in the organization aligns its measures to support the Six Ups. To make sure the teams are continuously measuring the variables most relevant to their success, these measures are reviewed annually against the organization's strategic goals and issues.

How to Make Sure They Mean What You Think

Invalid measures are worse than no measures at all, since they can lead to inappropriate decisions. The validity of measures is affected by the way they are selected, quantified, and reported. For example, one of our clients measures its accounts payable clerks based on the number of invoices they process. As its accounts became increasingly past due, however, vendors invoiced more frequently and also submitted duplicates, both of which made the team's performance look like it had improved, not gotten worse! Another client found that measuring and reporting the number of defects in its products was misleading because the opportunity to make a particular mistake varied significantly and correcting different defects had dramatically different costs. To prevent such distortions, teams should have significant input into defining measures for their work. Test and revise the measurements until they yield useful and easily interpreted data.

Which Measures to Consolidate

Certain measures will be important to the organization or PFU and others will be needed only within the team. For example, cost and customer satisfaction measures should be tracked at the team level, but then be consolidated with data from other groups to get a measure for the whole PFU. Equipment downtime probably needs to be tracked only at the team level. Measures that roll up should be tracked and reported in a consistent fashion so that they are comparable and easily consolidated. To this end, make sure you have clear definitions and consistent units of measurement. Consistency is not required for team measures. Again, as we discussed earlier, most attention should be levied on those measures that roll up to the PFU level.

Teams should track and report their own measures. In one organization, we built a team performance log that included the measures all teams were required to track. Then, for each measure, the log included a section on how to track, graph, and report it. Blank graphs were provided. We also included an appendix that showed them how to interpret data that were tracked for them (e.g., budgets and training hours).

Where certain measures are tracked for a team, the reports should be broken down to the team level and sent directly to the team rather than down through the traditional chain of command.

ENSURING A BALANCED SET OF MEASURES

Most organizations track a plethora of financial measures but have a dearth of customer- and employee-focused measures. Since all three elements should be optimized, it is important to create a balanced set of measures that will help you look into the future as well as review the past.

Steven Hronec of Arthur Andersen summarizes one such model in his book *Vital Signs* (see Figure 8–3). The matrix encourages an organization to measure cost, quality, and time at three levels: the organization, critical processes, and people. The recommended measures are listed inside the matrix. One advantage of this approach is that the second level, processes, builds joint accountability across functional boundaries. Even if your organization is not organized into PFUs, these process measures will encourage interdependent groups to cooperate.

Regardless of the model you use, the worksheet shown in Figure 8–4 may help you clarify your needs.

1. Analyze your mission as well as the strategic and operational plans to determine what measures will be critical to your knowing how well you are doing. You may need a combination of bottom-line, team performance, and team effectiveness measures. List these in the first column.

2. Determine how each measure will be tracked and reported: who will keep the records and which measures will be reported, how often the measure should be taken, what units will be measured, what computations should be performed (e.g., ratios, normalization, averages). Make appropriate notes in the next four columns.

3. Note any goals or acceptable ranges, if any.

FIGURE 8–3
The Quantum Performance Measurement Matrix

	Quantum Performance		
	Value		Service
	Cost	Quality	Time
Organization	Financial Operational Strategic	Empathy Productivity Reliability Credibility Competence	Velocity Flexibility Responsiveness Resilience
Process	Inputs Activities	Conformance Productivity	Velocity Flexibility
People	Compensation Development Motivation	Reliability Credibility Competence	Responsiveness Resilience

Reprinted, with permission of the publisher, from VITAL SIGNS by Steven M. Hronec, ©1993 Arthur Andersen & Co. Published by AMACOM, a division of the American Management Association.

FIGURE 8–4
Sample Team Performance Measures Worksheet

Measure	Organization Level	Frequency	Standard Unit	Method of Measurement	Goal or Acceptable Range (if any)
Customer satisfaction	Track at team level; report at PFU and organization	Quarterly	1–5 scale: 1 = Did not meet expectations 3 = Met expectations 5 = Greatly exceeded expectations	Customer surveys; random sampling of customers	3 or better
Self-directedness	Track at team level; report at managerial level	Semi-annually (Track for 3 years or until all teams are at least 75% self-directed)	Percentage of responsibility list tasks teams have assumed	Team audit by facilitators	No specific goals; expect each team to increase self-directedness during each measurement period
Productivity	Track at team level; report at PFU	Track daily; report monthly	Throughput of products per day (deduct any products not meeting customer specifications)	Computer-generated report	100% of schedule
Cycle time (temporary measure to track re-engineered work flow)	Track at team level; report at PFU	Track each customer order for the next month Do a random one-day audit once per quarter, after that for the remainder of the year	Hours and minutes	Log book	Reduce average cycle time to 3 days
Team effectiveness	Track at team level; not required to report	Do at least semiannually or as needed	Team assessment score (–2 to +2 on each dimension)	Team assessment survey	No specific goal; teams are expected to continuously improve their teamwork

FIGURE 8–4 (CONCLUDED)
Definition of worksheet categories:

Measure	A description of the measure you intend to use (customer satisfaction, meeting attendance, sales volume, etc.)
Organization level	The level of the organization where these data are collected and/or reported (team level, department level, plantwide, regionwide, etc.)
Frequency	How often the measure will be taken and/or reported (annually, quarterly, daily, etc.)
Standard unit	For quantifiable measures, the standard unit of measure to be used (percentage, total volume, dollar amount, revenue per employee, etc.)
Method of measurement	The means by which the measure will be taken (survey, interviews, sales records, time card records, expense records, etc.)
Goal or range	The desired results (100% accuracy, average score of 3.8 on a scale of 5, ±5% of budget, etc.)

CONCLUSION

Goals and measures, when properly designed and implemented, can be a powerful tool for building focused and accountable teams. When designing goals and measures, be careful to focus them at the appropriate level in the organization, and limit them to the few that are critical to your strategic issues. Involving teams in the design of measures as well as the collection and analysis of the data will provide them with the critical feedback they need in their pursuit of continuous improvement.

RECOMMENDED READING

Boyett, Joseph, and Henry Conn. *Maximum Performance Management: How to Manage and Compensate People to Meet Work Competition.* Macomb, IL: Glenbridge Publishing, 1988.

Hitchcock, Darcy. "The Engine of Empowerment." *Journal for Quality and Participation* 15 (March 1992), pp. 50–58.

Hitchcock, Darcy, and Marsha Willard. "Measuring Team Progress." *Journal for Quality and Participation* 15 (September 1992), pp. 12–18.

Hronec, Steven M. V*ital Signs: Using Quality, Time and Cost Performance Measurements to Chart Your Company's Future.* New York: AMACOM, 1993.

Rummler, Gary, and Alan Brache. *Improving Performance—How to Manage the White Space on the Organization Chart.* San Francisco: Jossey Bass, 1990.

Chapter Nine

How Do We Appraise and Reward Performance?

O rganizational systems are powerful predictors of personal behavior. In the previous chapter, we explained how goals and measures can support or detract from teamwork. Appraisals and rewards are equally influential. Unfortunately, most of our human resource systems are designed for the traditional manager-as-parent organization. These systems can represent significant barriers to team progress.

In this chapter, we explore the problems with traditional appraisal and reward systems and present practical alternatives. Since few organizations have reinvented their approach to these systems, some of the recommendations we share with you have not been tested in the courts. All we know is that existing systems are dysfunctional and destructive to teams. Each organization will have to invent its own unique solutions. At a minimum, we hope to share the guidelines and beliefs that should be used in redesigning your systems.

APPRAISALS: TAKING A PROBLEM AND MAKING IT WORSE

Traditional performance appraisals are an artifact of the traditional parental management paradigm. These systems typically involve three phases:

- Annual goal setting—manager and employee negotiate the goals against which the employee will be measured.
- Monitoring by the manager of the employee's performance throughout the year—the manager documents performance and gives informal feedback to the employee.

- Annual performance review—the manager rates the employee's performance against the goals and standards and reviews the employee's performance for the year. Often compensation is tied to this appraisal.

This process sounds so logical that it is hard to question. The problem is, it doesn't work; it is built on faulty assumptions. In this section, we explain what is wrong with this process and describe the misguided efforts to redesign it.

Why Traditional Performance Appraisals Destroy Teams

Traditional performance appraisals are based on the following assumptions:

- Managers are in the best position to assess an employee's performance.
- Managers are the only ones who should assess an employee's performance.
- Employee performance is determined primarily by competence and effort.
- Employees need to know where they stand and so should be ranked or rated.
- The manager needs to document everything in case he or she needs to terminate an employee.

All of these premises are false. Let's refute each one in order.

The first assumption, that managers are in the best position to appraise, reflects the father-knows-best paradigm. However, managers are often in a decidedly *poor* position to appraise an employee's performance. First and foremost, employees usually spend far more time with their co-workers and customers than with their managers. In addition, managers' knowledge of and experience with the technical details of the work are limited. Some have never performed the work, or technology and equipment have changed so much that managers' experience is outdated and irrelevant. Not only do managers appraise employees based on severely limited data; they can usually offer little technical assistance.

The second assumption, that the manager alone should judge performance, is clearly a violation of the inverted pyramid. It reinforces the notion that employees work for the boss; in a high-performance organization, employees work *with* others *for* customers. Therefore, peers and customers should be a primary source of feedback.

The third assumption places primary responsibility for performance on the employee. However, the late Edwards Deming asserted that systems determined approximately 80 percent of performance, not individual effort or skill. This is even truer in team settings where members are, by definition, interdependent. It is unfair to place 100 percent of the burden of performance on the individual. To make matters worse, the emphasis of these appraisals is usually on judging performance, not on problem solving, so little is done to fix the systemic barriers. Also, as we explained in the previous chapter, individual performance on the team should be treated as a private matter. Managers shouldn't muck about in the inner workings of a team unless the team asks for help.

The fourth assumption, that employees should be ranked or rated, is based on a misguided notion that competition improves performance and that providing a grade is the only clear way to give meaningful feedback. The thinking is that if I get a lower rating on my appraisal, I will be motivated to improve, to strive for the best rating, to outdo my peers.

It may seem like heresy to say this in the most competitive nation on earth, but competition rarely improves performance. Alfie Kohn, author of *No Contest: The Case Against Competition*, researched the issue thoroughly and found that instead of improving performance, competition usually impaired it. In addition, it had many nasty side effects:

- Competition necessarily makes losers, which leads to poor self-esteem. This reduced self-esteem often leads to a reinforcing cycle of wanting to compete more to prove oneself.
- Competition encourages people to view others as adversaries; this attitude becomes generalized, making people more distrustful.
- Competition creates artificial scarcity, for only so many can be rated as "exceptional." Scarcity increases competitive behavior, often leading to cheating, fudging the numbers, and justifying the means by the ends.
- Competition creates hostilities among groups and damages relationships. In cooperative settings, in contrast, people are more likely to understand diverse points of view and be more trusting and helping.

It is hard to build a team with distrustful, hostile, adversarial individuals with low self-esteem. As Kohn explains, cooperation is the antidote:

Performance ultimately suffers from competition just as it suffers from the use of any extrinsic motivator . . . . [T]o the extent that an extrinsic motivation *can* have a positive effect, one of the most powerful motivators is not money or victory but a sense of accountability to other people. This is precisely what cooperation establishes: the knowledge that others are depending on you.[1]

As we have said in previously published works, rating and berating are the same thing. You need not give someone a number or a label to help him or her improve.

The final assumption, that appraisals provide critical documentation, is a case of the tail wagging the dog. Most organizations want the documentation primarily to justify firing someone. While we have no data to support this notion, performance appraisals have probably been used *against* an organization as often as they have been used to support the organization's position. Furthermore, most organizations use progressive discipline practices that serve the purpose of justifying terminations, so using performance appraisals in this manner is redundant. The few other potential uses for performance appraisal data, such as for training needs assessment, can be fulfilled in other ways. Unfortunately, we have allowed our fear of the tiny minority of problem employees to dominate our use of our feedback system.

The purpose of the appraisal process should not be to keep your corporate attorney content. The purpose should be to help people reflect on the past and plan improvements for the future.

Multiplying the Mistake

Unfortunately, the most common modification made to performance appraisals in a team setting is to make everyone on the team perform the same abusive process on everyone else. Most team-based organizations have peers complete appraisal forms on every other team member and then let the manager deliver the verdict.

We have already made the case that traditional performance appraisals are based on inappropriate assumptions. Inviting peers into the fray solves only one of the problems: enlarging the source of feedback beyond just the manager. The other problems remain. So doing more of the same does not remedy the situation.

---

[1]Alfie Kohn, *No Contest: The Case Against Competition* (Boston: Houghton Mifflin, 1986), p. 67.

In addition, the traditional process is enormously time consuming. To do justice to the process, it takes at least several hours to prepare for and conduct the annual review, not to mention the time spent documenting performance throughout the year. Most human resource directors would like to see this process conducted quarterly so there will be no surprises. A manager with 20 employees who actually tried to carry out these guidelines could easily spend 400 hours, or 19 percent of his or her time, just conducting these appraisal sessions!

Some organizations, apparently addicted to management by gold stars and demerits, have employees rank or rate their peers. This practice is one of the most divisive and harmful to teams. In most organizations where teams rank order one another on various criteria, these practices have led to long-standing conflicts and rifts on teams.

THE TEAM IMPROVEMENT REVIEW[2]

Teams need regular feedback, but traditional appraisals don't work. So what is the solution? In other works, we have presented our "open appraisal" process in which the team, in an open setting, discusses answers to open-ended questions. We have found that the word *appraisal* is so fraught with negative connotations that we have abandoned it. We have also found that since the process fuses business planning and appraisals, the term is a misnomer, focusing on only one-half of the process. Since then, we have renamed it a *team improvement review*. Following are its foundation principles and steps.

The Principles of a Team Improvement Review

Merge planning and feedback. Managers and employees bristle at performance appraisals because the traditional process is laborious and disembodied from the core work. Instead of being tacked on as something extra, it should be integrated into how work gets done.

The solution is to merge business planning and performance appraisal into a single set of meetings. The entire work team should sit down regularly to reflect on the past and plan for the future. This approach

---

[2]This section includes excerpts from Mark G. Brown, Darcy Hitchcock, and Marsha Willard, *Why TQM Fails and What to Do About It* (Burr Ridge, IL: Irwin Professional Publishing, 1994).

transforms the meeting into an interactive team-building process while saving considerable time. Instead of conducting multiple individual meetings, the team and its manager hold one team meeting. Rather than a stilted meeting between manager and employees, these sessions resemble a regular team meeting in which team members reflect on their recent performance and make plans for the future.

Design the meeting around thought-provoking questions. The meetings should revolve around open-ended questions that inspire team members to think critically about their work and take ownership for their mini-enterprise. Often these questions fall into four sections:

- Past performance: What have been our accomplishments and problems?
- Future: What should our goals be?
- Developmental needs: What must we improve to meet our goals?
- Support needs: What support do we need from others to succeed?

Align the timing of the appraisal with the work. The frequency of the meetings should flow naturally from the work. For many organizations, aligning these sessions with fiscal periods works well. In these cases, a team might hold an extensive annual meeting to plan next year's goals and then meet quarterly to review performance and adjust the goals. Other teams may need a different schedule. Many jobs revolve around project work. In these cases, the meetings should be scheduled around milestones, with an extensive pre-project planning session and a post-project evaluation meeting. In some industries, such as tourism, teams may find it more appropriate to align their meetings to the seasons. Each work group should have the flexibility to adjust the timing of its meetings.

Eliminate individual ratings. Abolish all forms of individual ranking or rating including a 1 to 5 scale or terms such as "competent," "needs improvement," and the like. Ratings or grades provide no useful feedback. What is useful is feedback about the specific performance that led to the grade. The added step of translating observations into a score or rating contributes no value. It merely obscures what is important and wastes time.

Provide individual and team feedback.   Employees should receive feedback from multiple sources, not just the manager. In small teams, each person (including the manager) can receive feedback from all team members and, where appropriate, from customers. Larger teams (teams with more than eight people) sometimes devise ways to limit the time and number of sources of individual feedback so that the recipient isn't overwhelmed with input and the meeting doesn't drag on. In any case, these guidelines ensure a productive discussion:

- Let the recipients of the feedback evaluate their own performance before receiving comments from others. They should be encouraged to discuss strengths as well as areas for improvement. They should identify one focus area to work on for the next period.

- After a recipient evaluates himself or herself, team members add any number of comments about the recipient's accomplishments or strengths.

- Team members can either agree with the focus item or suggest one other item. If they suggest another, they should be able to provide a specific example of how to improve.

- The manager should generally receive his or her feedback last. Otherwise employees who raise sensitive issues might fear retribution.

In addition to individual feedback, time should also be devoted to discussing how well the team as a whole is operating.

Incorporate data about customers and competitors.   The team improvement review should compare the team's performance to the needs of the organization, not just those of the manager. Feedback from customers and about competitors is critical to the relevance of the review. In some cases, it may even be possible for customers to participate in the review process, as is often the case in project work. Alliant Techsystems' Marine Systems group, whose biggest customer is the U.S. military, has resident representatives who participate in team meetings so that the team has continual, direct input/feedback from its customer. Other options include using benchmarking data, customer surveys, focus groups, and performance measurement systems.

Design a natural way to document results.   As we explained in the previous chapter, teams should track their own performance measures on a regular basis. These measures should be reviewed in the team

improvement review during the first portion of the meeting, which
focuses on past performance. Whenever possible, let employees maintain
their own documentation. Partners shouldn't need someone to "keep
book" on each other.

As a work group refines this review process, a functional format
for documentation will emerge. For instance we at Axis refer (with
tongue in cheek) to our 9-P report: presentations, publications, promotions, prospects, proposals, projects, products, processes, and profits. This
structure, which embodies our corporate strategy, forms the agenda at our
review meetings and serves as a basis for documentation throughout the
year.

Individual feedback can be documented as part of the minutes of the
meeting or embedded in the process used to facilitate the individual feedback. In one organization, we designed the feedback process around
index cards. All team members documented their own strengths and areas
for improvement on the cards and then took notes as others shared their
feedback. These index cards were then filed away until the next review
meeting.

How to Conduct a Team Improvement Review

Follow these steps to prepare for and conduct a team improvement
review:

1. Explain to employees what the team improvement review is
   intended to do and the philosophy behind it.
2. Review with them the four major areas that should be discussed,
   and develop a list of questions for each area.
3. Establish ground rules for the meeting to ensure a positive
   outcome (e.g., addressing behavior, not personalities; leaving
   titles behind; etc.).
4. Make sure everyone has basic feedback skills. Provide communication skills training beforehand, or have a trained facilitator
   run the first sessions.
5. Provide all team members with copies of the questions at least a
   week before the meeting, and ask them to come prepared to discuss
   their ideas.

6. At the meeting, establish a comfortable atmosphere. Discuss each question at length, and come to consensus around future goals and tasks.

7. Establish a way to monitor your progress on important goals and tasks. Make sure responsibilities are clear. Whenever practical, leave it up to the individual team members to document their own performance against the team's goals throughout the year.

8. Wrap up the meeting with some form of celebration.

Lee Hebert, plant manager for Monsanto, has embraced the "open appraisal" concept for his team-based plant in Pensacola, Florida. Monsanto has discovered that sessions of three to four hours are optimal. If the team is not finished, it schedules another session to avoid burnout. It uses the same questions each time. One of Hebert's favorites is "If this were your business, what would you do?" because it builds ownership.

Here is how Hebert describes the benefits:

> The open appraisal process is a great vehicle for opening communication with the team. Position power is tough. People tend to tell you what they think you want to hear. So you have to be careful not to use your power to influence the direction of the discussion. But the open appraisal process gets the real issues on the table. Then we can see the possibilities and team members begin to see true growth opportunities.[3]

Hebert also notes that these team improvement reviews do not entirely eliminate the need for one-on-one sessions. When performance problems are raised during the meeting, he often follows up with individual coaching. His notes during the meeting serve as documentation. No individual ratings are given, which he believes helps employees see this as a developmental opportunity rather than a report card. While he thinks this process is far superior to traditional appraisals, he cautions that it has not yet been tested in the courts. As a trailblazer, he is willing to take the risk.[4]

Team performance is dependent on feedback. The problem is that most organizations have confused evaluation with feedback. When a team is given responsibility for tracking and monitoring its own performance, the focus naturally shifts from evaluation and blaming to data analysis and problem solving.

---

[4]Ibid. p. 117.

WHY PAY-FOR-PERFORMANCE (OR SKILLS, OR ANYTHING ELSE, FOR THAT MATTER) CAN'T WORK

Few management practices are based on as much misleading data as our compensation and reward systems. When asked, most managers will agree that they should "motivate and reward their people." Just as with performance appraisals, however, the basic premises on which managers act are inappropriate. In this section, we explain what's wrong with these fundamental assumptions.

Rats, Pigeons, and People

Virtually all reward systems in existence today are based on research with rats, pigeons, and other hapless, caged creatures. B. F. Skinner and other behaviorists discovered that if you reward an animal for a certain behavior, it is more likely to repeat the behavior. A hungry pigeon is placed in a cage with several levers. When it, by accident, pecks at one of the levers, a food pellet drops down. Soon the hungry bird is pecking away at the lever. Management theorists quickly deduced that if you want your employees to repeat certain behaviors, you should offer them rewards—money, recognition, promotions, and the like.

Unfortunately, what these studies say about our humanity isn't at all what we think we have learned. Not only is human behavior far more complex than that of a rat; employees are not in confinement, totally dependent on their master, despite how some may feel. Furthermore, in the studies it is difficult to discern what the animal is thinking about its situation, and the emphasis is on iterations and quantity, not the quality or creativity applied to the task.

What the Research Shows Rewards Do

If you review the research on Homo sapiens, you discover quite a different picture. In his insightful book *Punished by Rewards*, Alfie Kohn reviews this research. His findings are that rewards, which offer this for that, have the following effects:

- Rewards punish. Not getting an expected reward is indistinguishable in impact from punishment.

- Rewards rupture relationships. Those conferring the reward are necessarily sitting in judgment of the person receiving the reward, and thus are in a dominant position to him or her. Also, nothing generates more cynicism than watching a peer receive a reward she or he did not deserve.

- Rewards ignore reasons. Relying on the carrot to get behavior does nothing to get at the root cause if the employee cannot perform. As Kohn says, "In many workplaces, incentive plans are used as a substitute for management: pay is made contingent on performance and everything else is left to take care of itself."[5]

- Rewards discourage risk taking. Rewards shift the focus from the task to getting the reward, which encourages us to do as little as necessary to get the reward. Rewards also make us focus on quantity as opposed to quality.

- Rewards buy off intrinsic motivation and interest. We call this the "prostitution principle." It devalues the task in the eyes of the doer and increases the need for further rewards.

Kohn makes the case that typical approaches to verbal recognition are equally at fault. While it is permissible and appropriate for a manager to share specific feedback and information with an employee, if the manager is offering the recognition primarily to manipulate the employee's behavior, it is equally tainted.

Ironically, rewards do work. As Kohn puts it, "Do rewards motivate people? Absolutely. They motivate people to get rewards."[6] We don't think this was what managers had in mind when they created compensation systems!

HOW TO COMPENSATE TEAMS

The fact that rewards are immensely convenient and appear, at least in the short run, to do the trick makes them irresistibly attractive. If what we want, though, is dedicated, creative, and committed employees, certainly we must find a different way to handle compensation. In this section, we explore guidelines for a team-based compensation system.

---

[5]Alfie Kohn, *Punished by Rewards: The Trouble with Gold Stars, Incentive Plans, A's, Praise, and Other Bribes* (Boston: Houghton Mifflin, 1993) p. 16.

[6]Ibid., p. 67.

Sharing the Harvest

Imagine that you have a field to plant with corn. The traditional approach would be to hire some farmhands, give each a discrete task such as planting, watering, or harvesting, and offer to pay each for his or her task. Hired hands feel little responsibility to the ultimate outcome and, since each is asked to perform a discrete task, they would have little incentive to help each another.

Compare that approach to this one. Assemble a team of people and tell them, "Together we are going to raise a crop. First, we will buy the seed and tend the field. Then, when the crop is ripe, we will share the harvest." This is the feeling you want employees to have about your company. A noble and unifying vision is presented, and the rewards are shared fairly. Paying people should not be a bribe; it should be an equitable way to share in the harvest.

How, exactly, is this done?

Guidelines for Compensating Teams

All pay systems should be based on two fundamental principles:

- Positions should be compensated at their fair market value.
- The wealth should be shared equitably.

Following are some specific suggestions for enacting these principles.

To achieve the first principle, eliminate artificial differences in base pay. If employees question why Angie is paid more or less than Andy, perhaps the two should not be paid differently. Stop trying to make performance ratings justify arbitrary or accidental differences in employee pay. Similarly, eliminate discrepant reward systems for different layers of the organization. It is hard to preach partnership when your reward system delineates the lords from the serfs.

Partnership includes sharing the risks as well as the rewards. Sharing risk implies that everyone should have a variable pay component so that when the organization performs well, they all share in the wealth, and when it doesn't perform well, no one is artificially rewarded.

To share in the harvest, you must have a complete set of tasks, those that together produce an identifiable product or service. Remember the primary functional unit from the previous chapter? Base the variable portion of compensation on the performance of the PFU. Simple gain-sharing systems are our preference.

Stop flaunting the reward or compensation system. Set it up and let it go. Take down the thermometer charts showing how close the gain-sharing system is to its cap. For that matter, take off the cap.

This approach does not need to ignore individual star performers. For those occasions when individuals go above and beyond, have a system for giving individual rewards. These rewards should be tailored to the individual's interests and should never overshadow the group rewards. Give employees as much choice as possible about how and when these individual rewards are warranted. They should be a surprise after the fact, not a bribe for future performance.

Never turn rewards into a contest, pitting one group against another or limiting the number of teams that can earn the reward. The standards should be clear to everyone, and everyone who meets the standards should earn the reward.

CONCLUSION

In this chapter, we explained why traditional appraisal and compensation systems are damaging to teams. Unfortunately, few organizations have found entirely satisfactory replacements for traditional systems. To make matters worse, human resource directors, with their increasingly legalistic viewpoint, often present barriers rather than practical options. Their preference will be to tweak existing systems, but since these systems are based on inappropriate assumptions, this is patently not the answer.

Your organization will necessarily have to experiment and assume some risk to align these systems to support teams. Clarify the purpose of the systems and the fundamental beliefs they should support. Then build a new system from scratch. When people say, "It cannot be done," ask, "If it could be done, how would we do it?" Do not let old paradigms and legal anxieties determine the culture of your organization.

RECOMMENDED READING

Belcher, John. *Gainsharing*. Houston,: Gulf Publishing, 1991.

Brown, Mark G., Darcy Hitchcock, and Marsha Willard. *Why TQM Fails and What to Do About It*. Burr Ridge, IL: Irwin Professional Publishing, 1994.

Doyle, Robert. *Gainsharing and Productivity: A Guide to Planning, Implementation, and Development*. New York: American Management Association, 1983.

Hitchcock, Darcy. "Performance Management for Teams—A Better Way." *Journal for Quality and Participation*, September 1990, pp. 52–57.

Kohn, Alfie. "Why Incentive Plans Cannot Work." *Harvard Business Review*, September–October 1993, pp. 54–63.

Kohn, Alfie. *Punished by Rewards: The Trouble with Gold Stars, Incentive Plans, A's, Praise, and Other Bribes*. Boston: Houghton Mifflin, 1993.

Lawler, Edward, III. *Strategic Pay: Aligning Organizational Strategies and Pay Systems*. San Francisco: Jossey Bass, 1990.

Prince, J. Bruce. "Performance Appraisal and Reward Practices for Total Quality Organizations." *QMJ*, January 1994, pp. 36–46.

Swoboda, Frank. "At Motorola, Workers' Peers Have Say in Pay." *Washington Post*, May 24, 1994.

Zigon, Jack. "Making Performance Appraisal Work for Teams." *Training* 31 (June 1994), pp. 58–63.

Chapter Ten

Close Encounters with the Law

"We can't do that; it's against the law." When all other excuses fail, the law provides the final defense for those threatened by the change to self-direction. It's been an effective defense, too. For those of us who are not attorneys, it gives us pause. We certainly don't want to lay the organization open to any legal liabilities. But still we wonder, how real is this threat? Kim Fisher, best-selling author on teams, maintains that this legal threat is most often a smokescreen for other fears or concerns. It seems to be true. For every "legal" excuse we have encountered, we have been able to find an organization that somehow managed to overcome or work around it.

In this chapter, we look at some of the most intimidating legal excuses and describe strategies for proceeding with teams while keeping the organization out of hot water. Hiring and discipline, long the purviews of management, have often been held out of reach of teams on "legal" grounds. Job classifications protected by union contracts and civil service regulations are another obstacle that has kept organizations from achieving a fully flexible work force. Finally, there is the ultimate scare created by the National Labor Relations Board and its rulings on the Du Pont and Electromation complaints. What's an organization to do?

TEAMS AND HIRING

Among all the management responsibilities that are up for consideration as hand-offs, hiring seems to be the one that gets teams the most excited and management the most scared. From the team's perspective, it seems only logical and fair that it be able to pick the people with whom it will work. It should be clear by now that the most effective self-directed work teams are interdependent groups of people who must trust one another to pull together to achieve their goals. Who wouldn't want to have a say in who should make up that group?

For their part, managers worry that in an effort to build a harmonious group, teams will neglect issues of diversity that in some cases could end in a discrimination complaint. Personnel departments are quick to point out the dangers of letting inexperienced team members have control over the candidate review and interview process. One wrong question, even unwittingly asked, can land an organization in court faster than you can say, "Are you married?"

All of these concerns are certainly valid, but they are not insurmountable. Numerous organizations have successfully authorized teams to hire their own new members. Getting there, however, was seldom an overnight transition. At a northwest forest products company, early efforts at letting teams do their own hiring did in fact result in lots of employees with the same last names. To ensure a less biased approach and to protect itself from charges of nepotism, the organization contracted with an outside service to do initial screening of applicants.

Rather than limit the authority of the team, the Marion County Health Department in Salem, Oregon, ensured that the teams wouldn't make similar errors by educating them. It enlisted the county human resource office to help train team members on the ins and outs of interviewing and hiring. The training covered all the critical issues, such as establishing selection criteria, conducting interviews, checking references, and notifying applicants—the winner as well as the losers. Team supervisors enhanced this training with "just-in-time" coaching and technical troubleshooting.

For some teams, a measure of diversity training is appropriate as well. Each team needs to learn to strike a balance between creating a team on which everyone is in sync and creating a team that has enough different views, ideas, and styles to keep it creative and stimulating.

EARNING THE RIGHT TO HIRE

Even after thorough preparation, teams may still need to ride with their training wheels for awhile. Managers often think that empowerment means they must automatically and immediately trust teams to do the right thing. It's one thing to give teams the room to fail where the risks are small, but when it comes to hiring, where liabilities are greater, it is not unreasonable for managers to expect teams to earn their trust for this responsibility. Here again the EARN process described in Chapter Six has an application. As it applies to hiring, the scenario may go something like this:

Explain: In the first go-round, the manager explains how the process works and then lets team members watch. They are allowed to review the applications and sit in on the interviews and offer their comments.

Assist: The next time, team members share the job with the manager, contributing interview questions and perhaps even having a vote in the final decision.

Review: The third time, the manager reviews the process, perhaps critiquing selection criteria and interview questions beforehand, but giving the team the primary responsibility for the task. The manager just observes, stepping in only if the team gets into trouble or shows signs of violating the law.

Notify: Finally, the manager hands over full responsibility to the team and is only kept informed of its decisions.

This gradual hand-off gives everyone time to learn the process and build mutual trust and confidence.

TEAMS AND DISCIPLINE

Even among organizations that have comfortably handed off the hiring process, many have shied away from the issue of discipline. Most organizations don't even want to raise the subject. They are quick to point to their labor contracts, which stipulate that this is a management function. Push a little harder on this resistance and you quickly find the reluctance rooted in the teams' own discomfort with the issue. It's one thing to get to select whom you work with and quite another to have to confront your co-workers (and, in many cases, friends) when they aren't cutting the mustard. Many organizations have trouble envisioning a way to handle situations like performance problems other than taking on the parent role and either lecturing or punishing. No one likes to do that. At least managers are used to it. It's what they get paid the big bucks for, so the teams say.

Sometimes teams catch themselves in this contradiction. One team we worked with had been given the authority to hire and had recently added a new member. This new member was clearly not working out, though the problems were not raised openly in the team. The manager of the team felt pressured to do something about it because the new hire's probationary period was drawing to a close. He didn't think he had the time to involve the team in the process; anyway, it was still a management responsibility. The team was informed of the decision to let the new member go the day he was discharged. When we met with the team shortly afterward, the members seemed quite despondent. No one disagreed with the manager's decision, but they believed they had shirked their own responsibility: "We were the ones who hired him. We should have been the ones to have to deal with the problem."

They may have discovered an important point. Without the accompanying responsibilities, all the privileges are not true empowerment. Also, as pointed out in Chapter Nine, managers are not always in the best position to deal with performance problems within a team. We encountered another team at an automobile manufacturing plant that had a member with a substance abuse problem. The problem had been evident for years. Management had done the requisite counseling and referral to employee assistance many times with no effect. Finally, the team members confronted this individual with a very convincing message: "You come to work drunk. You work with a torch in your hand. We don't feel safe working next to you." A very powerful—and, in this case, eye-opening—message when it comes from your peers.

Mitigating the Discomfort

Admittedly, discipline and performance problems are about the stickiest issues with which teams must deal. One reason they are so difficult is that teams seldom have the mechanisms in place to systematically address issues before they become major problems. The Think Jet team at a Hewlett-Packard plant has handled its own interteam disciplinary issues for several years. It relies heavily on a structured process that has helped it accept this responsibility with few problems. When the going gets too rough and relationships are uncomfortably strained, team members call on their coach (whom they hired for themselves) to step in and help mediate discussions with a problem employee. The coach has no authority in the process. He or she only helps to facilitate and manage the potential conflict.

In the earlier example with the problem new hire, each individual on the team had had difficulties with the probationary member, but no system was in place for the team members to review and discuss together the performance of the new member. Each team member was left believing that she or he was the only one who had noticed a problem. They cut the hiring process short. They should have instituted a team performance review at one or two points early in the new hire's employment to head off problems. The story might have had a happier ending had they been more diligent about sharing feedback with one another, coaching the new member and helping him understand the team's goals and styles.

Peer review is perhaps the best antidote to situations that ultimately require discipline. Where team coaching and effective and timely feedback are in place (as in the team improvement review process described earlier), it is more likely that performance will be kept on track and that the need for disciplinary action will be greatly reduced.

Dealing with Contractual Limitations

Managing team issues and performance all along the way should head off many disputes or major problems. Where they do occur, some serious decisions need to be made. In many organizations, labor contracts specifically stipulate that discipline is strictly the responsibility of management. One team took the risky tack of taking on these responsibilities under the table. Team members had a tacit agreement among themselves not to tell, and the union would be none the wiser. This is a dangerous strategy. A labor contract represents a legal agreement between union and management. It deserves respect not only because of the legal ramifications but also because of the trust that is undermined when it is not respected.

Contracts, however, are often less inflexible than they seem. Some organizations review the contract in partnership with their unions and agree to broaden the interpretation of the clauses. Such was the case at the Marion County Health Department. A planning committee consisting of an equal number of managers and union representatives was created. Together they spent five days, using interest-based principles, negotiating parameters around hiring, firing, and the basic authorities of the supervisor. Without changing the collective bargaining agreement, they came to a set of mutual agreements around the interpretation of the contract's language dealing with management's discretion to delegate authority. The teams are now involved in hiring, budget writing, service performance monitoring, interpersonal problem solving, service delivery design, and training—all activities that *seemed* to be precluded by the contract.

TEAMS AND JOB CLASSIFICATIONS

Self-directed teams are defined by two basic characteristics: They have
the authority to make decisions for the good of the organization, and they
have the flexibility to act on those decisions in the service of the customer. This flexibility, the hallmark of the competitive organization, is
achievable only where jobs are broadly defined and team members are
crossed-trained and multifunctional. Many organizations, however, operate with job classifications that detail the functions of a job down to a
gnat's eyelash. How often have we heard the mantra "That's not my job; I
don't have to do that"? Unions have expended a great deal of energy to
achieve this level of detail to prevent organizations from exploiting workers. In the end, however, these agreements have hamstrung organizations
in their attempts to create responsive, outcome-focused teams.

Civil Service and Teams

Perhaps nowhere are job classifications as rigidly or narrowly defined as
in government civil service positions. As with union contracts, the origi-
nal intent was to protect workers against abuses like patronage hiring and
political manipulation. But like many good intentions, these regulations
have gone awry and turned into straitjackets for most agencies and
employees. In a survey of state managers conducted by the Massachusetts
Taxpayers Foundation, a government watchdog group, managers identified the civil service system as "the most serious impediment to accom-
plishing their mission." [1]

Bucking such a large and firmly entrenched system is more than most
organizations can handle. One county organization became so frustrated
with the constraints inherent in being a government agency that it peti-
tioned its county board of commissioners for a divorce. Publicly it said
the separation would enable it to compete for grants from private founda-
tions. The truth was, however, that it believed it could not create the kind
of flexible, customer-responsive organization it sought under the restric-
tive job classification system imposed by the state.

Divorce is not a viable option for many organizations, however. The
Civil Service Reform Act passed in 1978, though never fully exploited,

---

[1]David Osborne and Ted Gaebler, *Reinventing Government* (Reading, MA: Addison-Wesley,
1992), p. 1-25.

does make room for some beginning initiatives. The most notable effort was the China Lake Experiment conducted at the Naval Weapons Center in China Lake, California. As part of a major restructuring, the center collapsed some 18 GS (General Schedule) pay grades into no more than a half-dozen for each career path. These changes "allowed managers to pay market salaries to recruit people, to increase the pay of outstanding employees without having to reclassify them, and to give bonuses and salary increases based on performance."[2]

After successfully working through contractual issues with the union, the Marion County Health Department found itself confronted by the equally traditional county personnel system. The department wanted to redefine the role of supervisor to align with the values of self-direction. The role as it was traditionally defined no longer fit. The new role, as laid out in the department's rewritten description, called for coaching, consulting, and facilitating duties.

The personnel office, while sympathetic to the concepts, was hard-pressed to find anything in the definition that allowed it to justify the pay scale attributed to supervisors. In an effort to meet the requirements of the larger system without compromising its intent, the health department worked with the county personnel office to uncover the critical language necessary to maintain the pay grade. Ultimately it was the authority to hire that helped the personnel department justify the classification. While the teams at the health department actually have internal authority to interview and select their own team members, the supervisor still signs the official paperwork before it goes to the county to satisfy the rules. This solution may seem like a watered-down compromise that failed to shake up the outdated system, but when we examine how large-scale changes really occur, we find they generally begin with incremental learning steps like this one. Now that it is officially documented, how long can it be before the system begins to assume the pay grade is determined by all the other new duties now in the description?

EMPLOYEE INVOLVEMENT AND THE NLRB

In 1992 and 1993, the National Labor Relations Board (NLRB) ruled in two separate cases that the employee involvement committees at Du Pont

---

[2]Ibid., p. 128.

and Electromation Inc. were operating in violation of the National Labor Relations Act of 1935 and ordered them to disband. These decisions sent shock waves through America's most progressive and successful companies. How could efforts to increase the competitiveness of organizations and the job satisfaction of workers be illegal?

In the Electromation case, the NLRB decided that the five "action committees" established by the company to resolve employee displeasure with the company's new attendance and pay policies represented sham unions. The committees were composed principally of employees (selected by management from lists of volunteers) and one or two managers. Though the company was a nonunion environment, the Teamsters had been trying to mount an organizing drive at the site. It was they who filed the suit against Electromation in 1989.

For Du Pont, the troublesome spot was employer domination on seven panels set up to deal with safety and fitness issues. Because it salted the committees with managers who in effect had veto power over all the rank-and-file members of these panels, the company effectively froze the union out of discussions where it had a legally recognized interest and deprived employees of a bargaining agent loyal to their interests.

Whether these situations were created naively or with unscrupulous intent is neither clear nor relevant. What is important is to learn what we can from these cases so that we can steer clear of similar illegal practices. The intent of the National Labor Relations Act is to protect employees' right to bargain collectively with employers through representatives of their own choosing. This benevolent law, crafted in the 1930s, was in response to abuses perpetrated by some employers that had created employer-dominated "company unions." Unfortunately, the actual language of the law leaves a great deal open to interpretation. The sections of the National Labor Relations Act that pertain read as follows:

- Section 2(5) of the act loosely defines a labor organization as "any organization of any kind, or any agency or employee representation committee or plan in which employees participate and which exists for the purpose, in whole or in part, of dealing with employers concerning grievances, labor disputes, wages, rates of pay, hours of employment, or conditions of work."

- Section 8(a)(2) provides that it shall be an unfair labor practice for an employer to "dominate or interfere with the formation or administration of any labor organization or contribute financial or other support to it."[3]

The rulings and the law cause more concern for decision-making committees like steering groups or design teams than for the actual work teams. As indicated in section 2(5), any group, however small, can constitute a labor organization and can run into trouble if it begins discussing conditions of work. What topic of any relevance to a team would not fall under the definition of "conditions of work"? The law attempts to draw two main distinctions:

Business Issues		Bargaining Issues
Processes that deal with production or quality	versus	Processes that involve wages, hours, and other conditions of employment
Processes in which employees communicate information to management	versus	Processes that involve shared decision making and/or representation

It is the former situations in both distinctions that are permissible, while the latter ones begin to take an organization into treacherous legal waters.[4]

Though on the surface the rulings do not seem to support teams and empowerment, the members of the NLRB were quick to clarify that these decisions do not represent a broad condemnation of employee involvement. In their unanimous decision, the members of the board stated,

> These findings rest on the totality of the record evidence and they are not intended to suggest that employee committees formed under other circumstances for other purposes would necessarily be deemed "labor organizations" or that employer actions like some of those at issue here would necessarily be found, in isolation or in other contexts, to constitute unlawful support, interference, or domination.[5]

---

[3]Commission on the Future of Worker-Management Relations, *Fact Finding Report* (Washington, D.C.: U.S. Department of Labor and U.S. Department of Commerce, May 1994), p. 53.

[4]Ibid.

[5]Ned Hamsen, "Decision on Electromation Case by NLRB Does Not Directly Threaten Employee Involvement," *AQP Report*, February–March 1993, p. 2.

The labor laws upheld in these cases were intended to protect labor from unfair employment practices. However, what may have been relevant and critical in the 1930s, when they were written, begins to feel out of step in the 1990s. This anachronism has not gone unnoticed. In a *New York Times* article, labor secretary Robert Reich stated, "I'm absolutely convinced that we have to encourage organized labor and business leadership to move to a very different kind of compact than we have had in the past."

The Clinton administration has responded by creating the Commission of the Future of Worker-Management Relations, chaired by John Dunlop, former secretary of labor, to re-examine the laws and make recommendations for revisions. The commission is expected to make its recommendations by November 1994. As it can only recommend, we must ultimately rely on the decision processes of Congress to make any legal revisions. Given the speed with which Congress typically moves, most organizations will be eager to learn what they can do in the interim to ensure their competitiveness without violating the law. Concerned with how their decision would be interpreted, the members of the NLRB themselves have offered the following instructive guidelines.[6] (These guidelines are not meant to provide legal protection. Any organization should seek legal counsel where it has questions regarding these issues and fair labor practices.)

- Employers cannot coerce an employee to participate in any employee involvement program.
- If employees are representing other employees on a committee (like a steering committee or design team), they should be elected among themselves, not by the employer.
- Where unions are present, labor and management should have a clearly defined agreement on the workings, administration, and scope of any employee involvement effort. If the union chooses not to partner, the organization may need to limit the activity of any team to sharing information or making suggestions.[7]
- While the employer can establish the basic purpose for any committee, the committee should be free to consider any issues that are germane to that purpose.

---

[6]Ibid., pp. 2–4.

[7]This recommendation was actually issued by the board of directors of the Association for Quality and Participation.

- Management may participate on these committees, but may not dominate or wield undue power. The committees should also have the right to meet apart from management.

- Such committees would not be interpreted as a labor organization if they can be reasonably viewed as a vehicle for addressing employer interests (such as quality, customer service, process redesign, waste, and productivity) as opposed to employee interests (such as wages, benefits, safety, and working conditions).

- Employees must always be free to select traditional union representation and full collective bargaining.

Where the actual self-directed work teams are concerned, employers are probably safe if the following conditions are met:[8]

- Authority is delegated to the teams to make managerial operational decisions about their own work group.

- Employees do not have to deal with or negotiate over their decisions with management.

- No employee speaks as a representative for any other employee on collective bargaining issues.

CONCLUSION

Though legal issues are easily the most intimidating obstacles teams will face, we hope organizations will not raise up the white flag too quickly. Too many organizations have successfully overcome these issues for others to be completely discouraged by them. While the suggestions presented in this chapter should not be construed as legal advice, we hope it inspires creative ideas for legitimately pursuing self-direction.

RECOMMENDED READING

Commission on the Future of Worker-Management Relations. *Fact Finding Report*. Washington, DC: U.S. Department of Labor and U.S. Department of Commerce, May 1994.

---

[8]Debra Kolodny, "Tips on Keeping Participation Efforts Legal," (Conference Proceedings, Association for Quality and Participation), Spring 1994, pp. 528–30.

Fadem, Joel. "Employee Involvement Illegal? An Update." *Work Design Network News* 3 (February 1993), pp. 1–3.

Fisher, Kimball, Steven Rayner, and William Belgard. *Tips for Teams*. New York: McGraw-Hill, 1995.

Levinson, Marc. "Playing with Fire." *Newsweek*, June 21, 1993, pp. 46–48.

National Labor Relations Board. Decision of NLRB in E. I. Dupont & Co. Washington, DC: The Bureau of National Affairs, June 8, 1993.

Osborne, David, and Ted Gaebler. *Reinventing Government*. Reading, MA: Addison-Wesley, 1992.

Chapter Eleven

The Immune Response

M any organizations work hard to get some successful teams up and running only to find that the rest of the organization sabotages them. We liken this phenomenon to the immune response of the human body. Like the white blood cells that seek and destroy alien intruders, so too may other parts of the organization not involved in the implementation of self-direction attempt to thwart the efforts of a successful team. Some of these problems result from the lag time incurred when a whole organization does not progress at the same rate. Even in organizations where the implementation is done all at once—as opposed to being done in pilot groups—progress is rarely even and steady. Those parts that lag behind can frequently take on the job of the white blood cells.

In this chapter, we examine several different types of immune reactions common to organizations. The first deals with those situations in which individuals or groups exhibit a defensiveness in response to the changes going on around them. These "bucket draggers" can seldom completely derail an effort by themselves, but they can cause considerable drag and discomfort. Another phenomenon that diminishes the impact of self-direction is the organization's inability to share the learnings from one team to another. Instead of creating interdependencies and synergies, some organizations simply end up with new and different fiefdoms. Last are those situations in which large parts of the organization have been untouched by the move to self-direction and their lack of understanding for the new style inhibits the rest from realizing their potential.

PEOPLE TRIPPING YOU UP

For many people, the implementation of self-directed work teams is a realization of what is natural and easy. Some, however, are threatened by such a radical change; they get defensive in the face of the new styles of behaving and resist the conversion. Robert Hershock, group vice president at the division of 3M that makes respirators and industrial safety equipment, encountered this type of opposition when he began developing self-managed "action teams." One manager in particular was a real impediment. Typical of most naysayers he vociferously complained about the new ideas generated by the action teams, but was unwilling to propose any alternatives of his own. He actually told his staff, "Meet with the action teams because Hershock said so, but don't commit to anything. Just report back to me what was said." [1] Hershock tried unsuccessfully to convince the manager of the benefits to be realized from the changes being implemented. Eventually the manager became so uncomfortably out of step that he transferred to another part of the organization.

What You Can Expect

Experience has shown us that only about 3 to 5 percent of any organization's population will fall into this "over my dead body" category. In almost every case they, like the manager at 3M, eventually go away of their own accord. A significantly larger percentage of people, however, take their time coming around to the new way of operating. These are the people who deserve patience and nurturing, because we have found in the end that many of them will become the greatest enthusiasts. At a chemical plant, we met a team member who flatly refused to participate in "this team crap." The other team members continued to invite him to all their meetings, but wisely did not insist on his participation. Over time, he began to poke around at the meetings on his own. The last time we visited this team, we were pleasantly surprised to see this worker actually facilitating the meeting.

Strategies for "Bucket Draggers"

As implied, the most effective strategy is to give these people the time and space to come around at their own speed. Invite them to participate, but let them watch from the sidelines for awhile. Honor their experience and knowledge. Though self-direction requires a change in behavior of nearly everyone, be sure that those who are slower to adapt don't feel as

---

[1] Brian Dumaine, "Who Needs a Boss?", *Fortune*, May 7, 1990, pp. 54–55.

if this change invalidates everything they have done in the past. As much as possible, let them watch their peers who are modeling the right behavior. Offer them all the help and encouragement they need, while at the same time reinforcing the message that eventually they will be expected to "get on board."

The Clackamas County Department of Transportation and Development recently began to implement teams among the road crews responsible for building and maintaining the roads in this rapidly growing suburb of Portland, Oregon. This organization had long embraced the "just do your own job" attitude. The intent was to create teams that would take responsibility for their own outcomes and be mutually accountable for achieving team goals. Logically this implied cross-training and deploying crew members to whatever task was called for at the time. This effort violated the long-standing union system of classifying workers. Most of the crew members objected vehemently to "working out of class." "I put in my time as flagger; I don't do that anymore" was the common refrain.

One crew didn't see it that way. It began taking the initiative to see that the job got done even if it meant that a class IV worker (equipment operator) flagged or cut brush. The rest of the crews snubbed this team. They would not speak with the team members in the break room. When this self-directed crew had an opening, it asked for and was granted the authority to select the new member. It posted a "want ad" in the department inviting other employees to "interview" for a position on the team. Many of the other road workers were insulted by the prospect of being interviewed by "lower-class" workers and boycotted the selection process.

Wisely Dave Phillips, the department's manager, did not push the issue. He did slowly expand the team concept so that now teams form and reform each season to match the level and type of work done. Each team has a core set of members who are carryovers from the previous season. These members are then allowed to fill the remaining team slots from among the available employees who have signed up. Not surprisingly, those employees who have been unwilling to be flexible in their job assignments are frequently not chosen for a team and end up on the "extra" crew—the least desirable position in the department.

Though still in its experimental stages, the department has already realized two positive results from this system. First, the crews are breaking all records for productivity. They have reduced their costs by as much as 30 percent in some cases, doubled the number of miles of road they paved over the previous year, and at the same time increased the quality and durability of their product. The other notable result is in the performance and attitude of the "bucket draggers." Phillips reports that his two lowest performers (both of whom ended up on the extra crew this season) are now willing to do anything just to be part of one of the teams.

TEAMS DON'T LEARN FROM ONE ANOTHER

Most organizations understand the benefits of creating cross-functional teams. When teams are organized around a whole entity—a process, product, project, or customer—and all the expertise relating to that whole is present on the team, the result is almost always an improvement in decision making, flexibility, quality, and productivity. The interdependencies of the members of such teams becomes evident, sometimes for the first time. Where before people lived in functional towers, they now work side by side on common problems and issues.

It is this interdependency that unleashes the power of shared goals and mutual accountability. Such "horizontally" designed organizations are much more interdependent than functional ones, making it critical that teams practice systems thinking and ensure that team learnings are shared and distributed throughout the organization. Too frequently, though, teams become overly focused on their own goals, leaving open the possibility of disconnects and rivalries among the teams. At a lumber mill in the Northwest, two product teams became so obsessed with their own goals that they suboptimized the larger organization. One team was responsible for milling A-grade lumber, and the other team produced wood chips used in the manufacture of particleboard. In an effort to outproduce the other team, the chip team began grinding up A-grade lumber!

A similar situation arose at Dynamix, Inc., an interactive computer games producer in Eugene, Oregon. The nature of its business made project teams a natural structural option. Teams formed around a particular software product, seeing it through from creative inception to its debut on the market. Once a program is finished, team members disband and are redeployed to other product teams. The teams not only succeeded in producing very creative and innovative products, they were equally successful at problem solving in the design process. The teams' technical programming advisors, for example, frequently modified the programming software to make it easier for their team programmers to design the specific features of the game they were working on. The flaw was that these modifications were not shared across the organization. This became particularly problematic when the team disbanded and the members separated to form various new teams. Every time a programmer joined a new team, she or he encountered a different and unfamiliar version of the software. To make matters worse, the technician who designed this version was not even on the same team. The result was confusion and an overdependence on the knowledge of just a few of the self-created experts.

Formalizing Team Links

While the basic team structure and design at Dynamix worked well for product development, the linking structures among teams were missing, and creating confusion and inflexibility. To remedy the problem, the organization created connecting teams that it called "peer spheres" (the equivalent of star points), made up of the functional position members of each team. There was, for example, an engineering sphere, a production sphere, an arts sphere, and a creative services sphere. These groups met periodically to share learnings and software modifications to maintain consistency in technology and diffuse innovations quickly throughout the organization.

Formalizing a linking structure is one way to facilitate cross-team coordination. Other organizations have used less formal and more creative ideas to achieve this outcome. One of Monsanto's plants, for example, held what it called a quality fair, where each team put up a booth displaying its achievements, innovations, and learnings. In a similar vein, the first teams at Bell Atlantic held open houses to explain to others in the organization what they were doing and why. While still CEO of Johnsonville Foods, Ralph Stayer instituted an elegantly simple learning tool that involved having employees scan, clip, and review periodicals.[2]

Turning the Structure on Its Head

While formalized infrastructures such as these can contribute to the ability of an organization to share information freely, sometimes the abolition of structure is necessary. Such was the strategy at Oticon, a 90-year-old

---

[2]James Belasco and Ralph Stayer, *The Flight of the Buffalo: Soaring to Excellence, Learning to Let Employees Lead* (New York: Warner Books, 1993), p. 129.

Danish hearing aid manufacturer. Lars Kolind, who took over as president in 1988, believed that nothing short of a revolution was necessary to achieve flexibility and advance knowledge in the organization.[3]

Oticon, which competes in an industry against such giants as Siemens, Philips, and Sony, was woefully positioned. Kolind tells a story of having discovered that the company invented the first fully automatic hearing aid in the mid-1980s, but the idea was buried and effectively lost to the organization by poor interdepartmental communications.[4]

Kolind shook the organization to its core with a four-pronged strategy. First, departments and job titles disappeared. Jobs were reconfigured into fluid categories that leveraged each employee's special skills and personal goals.[5]

Second, all work was centered around projects initiated and implemented by informal groups of employees. These projects emerged "chaotically" by design. As many as 100 major projects are going at one time, none of which operate under controls or restrictions for allocating resources. The philosophy is, as Kolind phrases it, "If you're in doubt, do it. If it works, fine. If not, we forgive you."[6] Results have garnered Oticon 23 percent growth and a 25 percent increase in profits despite a generally declining market.

Third, the traditional office layout was abolished and replaced with drawerless electronic workstations. Informal dialogue replaced interoffice memos and E-mail. All incoming mail was scanned into the computer and then shredded. Coffee bars and "dialogue rooms" were scattered throughout the building to encourage informal meetings. Kolind discouraged the use of elevators because people were more likely to talk to one another as they passed or climbed the stairs. Important facilities were placed at the corners of the buildings to give people the opportunity to visit every part of the office. The very clearly conveyed message? It is much more important to talk to your co-workers about what to do than to hide behind a cubicle. Kolind is convinced that "oral communications is 10 times more powerful, more creative, quicker and nicer" than any other form of communication, including E-mail.[7]

---

[3]Polly LaBarre, "The Dis-Organization of Oticon," *Industry Week*, July 18, 1994, pp. 23–28.

[4]Ibid.

[5]Ibid.

[6]Ibid., p. 26.

[7]Ibid.

Fourth, as part of this radical new design, a transition team created an informal training mechanism that involved giving every employee a workstation like the ones planned for use in the new facility to take home on the condition that he or she would agree to self-train. Employees leaped at the opportunity. They not only did the self-learning on their own time but also created a "PC club" to support one another's learning. Another side benefit was that having workstations at home eroded the traditional concept of working hours and created a much more flexible, self-directed approach to work.[8]

All these changes were based on three philosophical beliefs about how to connect work groups and facilitate organizational learning:

- Choice—employees choose their projects. Workers who fail to seek out projects and opportunities do not last long at Oticon.
- Multijobbing—instead of a traditional hierarchy, Oticon has a network of experts. Employees are encouraged to include something in their job roster for which they think they aren't qualified. This strategy allows them to indulge their curiosity and broaden their expertise.
- Transparency—every piece of information is available to everyone.

Though Oticon had the luxury of building a new facility that incorporated all of these amenities, most are ideas that any organization could employ. The biggest obstacles are not our physical facilities as much as our assumptions about what constitutes "work."

THE REST OF THE ORGANIZATION THINKS YOU'RE WEIRD

Sometimes organizations get distracted by the success of the teams that are up and running and forget to attend to those portions of the organization that have not been converted. Sometimes, while no one is looking, these other parts begin to mount their defenses in an attempt to protect the status quo.

We see this phenomenon most frequently in American companies owned by European corporations. A southern manufacturer was two years into its implementation before its French parent company got impatient

---

[8]Ibid.

for results and began pouring cold water on the effort. A California plant owned by a famous Italian tire manufacturer had already realized significant gains when Italy got wind of the radical practices the company had implemented and replaced the plant manager with a very traditional one from corporate who reversed most of the changes. A German-owned high-tech manufacturer has thus far been allowed to pursue self-direction. The condition is, however, that this "experiment" will be condoned only as long as the plant maintains its current profitability, which it reports monthly.

While distance and cultural differences may account for the lack of understanding and support in some companies, we have also seen similar resistance come from right next door. A number of organizations we have encountered have had pilot teams in place for some time—long enough, in most instances, to have demonstrated significant gains. In spite of their successes, the most frequent reaction from the rest of the organization is one giant yawn.

In one situation, a department of a Northwest utility company had taken advantage of its semiautonomous status to implement some innovative practices. As is typical, it eventually bumped up against some of the organizational systems. In this case, it wanted to implement a pay-for-skills compensation system. The corporate compensation department initially gave the OK, but then later implemented a new electronic payroll system that didn't accommodate tracking the program in effect at the departmental branch site. While the department was not forbidden from continuing, it was not supported, and the program died from complications.

Sometimes the reaction goes beyond indifference to out-and-out resentment. A team of telephone service representatives at Bell Atlantic in Silver Springs, Maryland, encountered this sentiment. Though the team had been empowered with many of the responsibilities formerly held by its manager, it found that other managers refused to do business directly with the team because it lacked the appropriate "rank."[9]

The solution to this problem is not unlike the tack suggested earlier for dealing with individual bucket draggers. When you lack the needed support of other parts of the organization, your best strategy is to slowly begin to expose them to what you are doing. Teach them without con-

---

[9]Beverly Geber, "Guerrilla Teams Friend or Foe?", *Training* 31 (June 1994), pp. 36–39.

fronting them. Share your success and learnings, being careful not to show them up. Involve them in your processes. If there is no logical role for them to play directly, ask for their advice or opinions. Give them time to watch and make up their own minds. Let your results do your proselytizing.

Tact and diplomacy may be the most important skills in these situations. One government agency administrator found himself in a very delicate position. The innovations he and his teams had implemented had drawn a lot of attention from his governing board as well as from his peers from other agencies. He kept constant watch on their reactions. While he felt the need to share his experiences so others who wanted to go this route could learn from his mistakes, he also understood that absorbing too much of the spotlight was not a politically astute move.

Another team coach took a more assiduous but effective tack. He conducted a slow and steady assault on the rest of the organization by continually widening the scope and membership of his team, one person at a time. Each added "outsider" was brought into the team either as a full member or in a consultative role. This gave the newcomers a prime opportunity to watch and learn. In the end, they became "missionaries" for the team in other parts of the organization.

CONCLUSION

As the evidence suggests, having a good idea, even one with proven results, isn't always sufficient to overcome organizational inertia and entrenched policies and structures. For self-direction to thrive, however, organizations need to implement strategies that build connections among teams, facilitate the free flow of information, and produce irrefutable results. These strategies, coupled with patience, are the best weapons in the battle with this immune response.

RECOMMENDED READING

Bridges, William. "The End of the Job." *Fortune*, September 1994, pp. 62–74.

LaBarre, Polly. "The Dis-Organization of Oticon." *Industry Week*, July 18, 1994, pp. 23–28.

Peters, Tom. *Liberation Management: Necessary Disorganization for the Nanosecond Nineties*. New York: Alfred A. Knopf, 1992.

Senge, Peter, Charlotte Roberts, Richard Ross, Bryan Smith, and Art Kleiner. *The Fifth Discipline Fieldbook*. New York: Currency, Doubleday, 1994.

Wick, Calhoun, and Lu Stanton León. *The Learning Edge*. New York: McGraw-Hill, 1993.

PLEASE SEND MORE INFORMATION ABOUT

❏ PARS   ❏ Membership
❏ Education Courses   ❏ Conferences
❏ *The Journal for Quality and Participation*

Name_____ Title_____

Company_____

Address_____

City, State, Zip_____

Phone_____ Fax_____

AQP
Association for Quality and Participation
801-B West 8th Street • Cincinnati, Ohio 45203
(513) 381-1959 • Fax (513) 381-0070

BUSINESS REPLY MAIL

FIRST CLASS MAIL   PERMIT NO. 16494   CINCINNATI OH

Postage Will Be Paid By Addressee

AQP **ASSOCIATION FOR QUALITY**
AND PARTICIPATION
801 B WEST 8TH STREET
CINCINNATI OH 45203-9946

Chapter Twelve

Bait 'n Switch

E ven if you've managed to skirt most of the problems identified in the previous chapters, you may not be home free. The sorrowful truth is that even if you've followed all the rules and kept your own house clean, you may still be victim to forces out of your control. If you've ever spent the afternoon raking your yard clean only to have a gust of wind cover your lawn with your neighbor's leaves, you know the futility of battling the fates. You may rail against the injustice, but the leaves don't go away.

Unfortunately, when faced with such cruel twists of fate, too many organizations, out of fear, confusion, or weakness, revert to old, familiar practices. Those members of the organization who had put faith in the new partnering agreement feel deceived and disillusioned. Like the old bait 'n switch scam, employees believe they've been lured into the store with the promise of something great, only to be sold the same old junk. This violation is all too common.

Most written contracts include a clause stating that the terms and conditions cannot be changed without mutual consent. Furthermore, the contractual parties *and* their assigns are bound by the agreement. Transferring your interest in a contract to someone new does not absolve that party of the responsibility to abide by its terms.

When you ask your employees to become partners, the same rule should apply to the implied employment contract. Leaders should not stage a coup and seize employees' rights. However, this is in fact exactly what happens in many organizations.

Of the myriad problems teams can face, this bait 'n switch is by far the most damaging. Employees are enticed into sharing responsibility and then, when conditions change, their powers are stolen. More than any other problem, this can unravel all the progress made and make it more difficult to begin again.

This contract violation occurs most frequently in two situations. The first is when a change in leadership occurs that leaves the organization without its champion. The second occurs when market changes or financial setbacks send people scurrying for safe harbor. While we don't have the magic wand that will hold the fates at bay, we do offer some suggestions for preparing yourself for these eventualities.

CHANGES IN LEADERSHIP

Leaders leave for many reasons. They may retire, quit, be promoted, or even die. This loss always introduces a certain degree of turmoil in any organization. However, this turmoil is not the primary problem for teams. What really throws teams off track is a change in philosophy that often accompanies new leadership.

Can This Partnership Be Saved?

When a key leader must be replaced, some organizations forget to make empowerment one of the key selection criteria. For example, in the 1980s a steel mill on the West Coast, faced with severe competitive pressures, upended its traditional relationship with employees by making them partners. Three influential leaders set in place powerful systems to support this change. The organization became an ESOP, giving employees ownership of the company and including them in a profit-sharing plan. In addition, the organization developed a "peer review" process. This is not an appraisal process, as the name might imply, but a pseudo-judicial appeals system to resolve significant disputes as in the case where employees feel they have been unfairly treated.

These changes created a dramatic turnaround, and the organization was held up as a model for others to follow. Unfortunately two of the three leaders soon retired. The third became chairman of the board, far removed from daily operations. A traditional, controlling manager was promoted into a key leadership role. When someone suggested to this new plant manager that employees expected fair treatment, his response reportedly was "Fair! If they think I have to be fair with them, they'll think they're running the place." Need we say more?

Since that time, the organization has backslid in many areas. Managers within the plant who would like to be empowering are afraid to do so for fear of repercussions. Because terminated employees sold their stock on the open market, remaining employees no longer own a controlling share of the organization. Employees who remain are disgruntled, and the atmosphere is depressing.

This is clearly a violation of the partnering employment contract. Employees were given power, but only for as long as it served the needs of the organization to lift it from the jaws of bankruptcy. Then their power was brushed aside like a pesky gnat. The bitterness and mistrust this engendered may never be undone, for the seasoned veterans will share their oral history with all new recruits. If the organization once again needs the additional energy of its employees, it may get the cold shoulder. Only decades or a dramatic overhaul of leadership can restore this organization to its previous potential.

Using a Traditional Selection Process

Many organizations that have adopted partnering continue to use a traditional selection process. The new leader is selected without input from the employees. It never even occurs to many executives to involve employees in the selection of their leader. This increases the likelihood that the new leaders will not be a good fit with the culture of the organization.

Why shouldn't employees have a say in the selection of their leaders? When employees are given this power, they have a vested interest to make the new leader successful. Personally, we'd bet on the average leader who has the support of all the employees over a gifted leader who lacks that support.

If allowing employees the right to select organizational leaders is too radical, perhaps a more palatable strategy is to include the organization's steering committee in the selection process. Presumably this group, which is strongly invested in the implementation and maintenance of teams, will advocate for candidates who can support the teams' efforts and philosophies.

These ideas emphasize the need to define the selection criteria based on the values of self-direction and the needs of the teams. Human resources can still provide invaluable assistance in screening applicants, but they and other executives shouldn't necessarily have sole authority for the decision.

Mergers, Takeovers, and Other Hostile Acts

Mergers and acquisitions represent a special case of losing leadership. Often most of the leadership leaves en masse. One aerospace contractor on the West Coast was making great strides toward self-direction until it was abruptly taken over. Employees who were used to running their own show were now expected to adhere to a company-defined dress code. Radios were banned from the office space. Almost all of the respected leaders were called one by one into a conference room to be fired and then escorted out of the building. Strong ties were snapped without so much as a good-bye. The return of a functional, structured, autocratic environment left most employees reeling.

Six months later, the organization claims to have increased its profitability, though employees no longer know this for sure since financial data, once freely shared, are now kept secret. The organization seems to have too readily traded short-term gains for long-term investment. Turnover has been high and will be higher as soon as the local economy allows a disgruntled work force to jump ship. Also, the organization's earlier attempts to diversify its markets and achieve the kind of flexibility that should sustain it long term in a very volatile industry have all but been abandoned. The remaining managers are permitted to manage in a team fashion as long as they don't bother anyone. In the end, most of the teams are slowly dying from lack of attention.

How to Ensure a Lineage of Leadership

We know of no partnerships in which an active partner can assign his or her interest to another party without the consent of the other active partners. If you are serious about partnering with your employees, the same restrictions should apply. The following five recommendations will help ensure that future leaders abide by the terms of the partnering agreement.

1. Develop a participative selection process. Before a leadership position becomes vacant, agree on a participative selection process. This can take many forms. At a minimum, employees should have input into the selection criteria and their relative weight. They may, through representatives, participate in the selection process by reviewing résumés and interviewing candidates. It is also possible to let all employees vote on their new leader, as done in ESOPs via proxy statements.

Where boards of directors select new leaders, ensure that they are educated about self-direction and the kind of experience and philosophy needed to support it. Add credibility to this education with data showing the gains the organization has made with teams. If the teams have not been in place long enough to have results of their own, share the data about achievements of other, preferably similar organizations. Build the business case for your ideas, and secure an agreement to adhere to it.

2. Make a partnering management philosophy a BFOQ. If a participative, empowering style can be made a bona fide occupational qualification (BFOQ), include it in the job description and selection criteria. Experience may tell only part of the story, however. You should also make a point of testing candidates' reactions to certain situations to determine if their credentials and espoused beliefs are genuine.

3. Document the philosophy and employment contract. Several organizational leaders have written books in preparation for their departure. Ralph Stayer, owner of Johnsonville Foods, wrote *Flight of the Buffalo*. Les Schwab, owner of a customer-obsessed tire distributor, wrote *Pride in Performance*. Such books provide lasting guidance long after the leader departs. They document the beliefs and philosophy underlying the organization.

In addition, organizations may want to find other ways to codify the rights and responsibilities of their members. An organization can write an employee bill of rights for all of its members. A decision-making council with representation from all levels of the organization can be formed to handle strategic issues. Formalizing participation in various systems, such as in strategic planning, can also be helpful. Unions can also help keep management honest in its actions. Written documents and formal procedures help prevent new leaders and owners from usurping power.

4. Imbue the cultural history with partnering myths, stories, heroes, and symbols. A leader can also plant a legacy through oral history and organizational symbols. For better or worse, employees tell and retell stories about critical incidents in the organization's history. It is important to make sure that the core events in these stories support partnering. As with any oral history, the stories tend to become more mythical and exaggerated over time, but the moral is usually preserved. By telling stories that exemplify partnering and through dramatic and symbolic actions, a leader can help preserve the organization's culture.

5. Groom the next generation of leaders. Promoting from within is not always appropriate, but doing so provides many more opportunities to influence the outcome. This is especially true where organizations have made a significant investment in training their managers and supervisors.

TOUGH TIMES

Organizational crises represent golden opportunities to renew a commitment to partnering. Unfortunately, panic often makes many organizations revert to old parenting behaviors. Ironically, this represents the exact opposite of the steel company example mentioned at the beginning of this chapter where hard times prompted management and employees to *become* partners. The message is, never become complacent.

Contrasting Examples

One major telecommunications company fell into this trap. Up until the early 1990s, we referred many organizations to this company as a superlative example of union–management cooperation in implementing self-directed teams. It carefully laid the foundation for teams through written agreements, and practically everything was done in union–management pairs. The organization validated the union's right to exist by showing it as one corner of a stakeholder triangle, the other two corners being the organization and the employees.

Then, in 1991–92, the organization's team efforts took a double hit. First, it lost the leaders who had sponsored the self-directed team activity. They were replaced by other directors who did not believe in this style of management and wanted to eliminate the differences that had been created among the offices. Later, when the company announced its massive layoff plan in the face of competitive pressures, the efforts all but came undone. Today only a few corners within the corporation exhibit any recognizable vestiges of self-direction.

We have seen similar knee-jerk reactions to crises in other organizations as well. Sometimes, however, it is the employees that violate the partnering agreement. A forest-products company based in the Northwest was making steady progress in empowering its employees. The employees and their union had been granted significant authority for running the mills and making day-to-day business decisions. They were proving themselves good at it too, at least while times were favorable. When market changes and timber shortages created some financial setbacks for the organization, though, the unions began to feel threatened by the insecure environment and started to make decisions in their own best interests. A few poor decisions sent everyone back to their corners and the comfort of the old, familiar, traditional roles. While not all ground was lost, the experience taught everyone some hard-earned lessons about partnering.

Compare these cases to Alliant Techsystems' Marine Systems group, a defense supplier that manufactures torpedoes, antisubmarine warfare (ASW) systems, and other products it couldn't tell us about. Since the end of the Cold War, the defense industry has been devastated. To make matters worse, Alliant was spun off from Honeywell at a time when major contracts were being terminated. Its plant near Seattle now has approximately one-third the number of employees that it had three years ago.

Alliant Techsystems credits its success under such difficult circumstances to the following:

- It had a champion. Upper management was squarely behind teams, the team concept, and empowerment.
- While layers of management were cut, key members (including the champion) remained on staff to carry out the vision. These people had a long-standing relationship with and the *trust* of employees.
- It was tenacious in its pursuit of partnership. It firmly believed teams were a critical component in its survival plan.
- Despite difficult economic conditions, it preserved significant funds and resources for training.

How to Be Partners during Tough Times

Your organization will likely experience a crisis sometime in the future: an economic downturn, loss of a key customer, deregulation, a major accident, product tampering, lawsuits, natural disasters. Pick your poison. Before the inevitable happens, during more sane and sanguine times, decide how these crises will be handled so that the values of partnering are maintained.

Leadership, clear responsibilities, and reliable channels of communication are critical in any emergency. Provide for these with partnership in mind. Managers shouldn't be the only leaders, the only ones calling the shots, and the only ones with current information.

Devise an efficient mechanism for making decisions that includes representation from all levels and areas of the organization. For example, one communications networking manufacturing firm has succeeded in establishing a representative structure for ensuring participative decision making. Its steering team is composed of representatives (both salaried employees and bargaining unit employees) from each of the organization's departmental steering teams. Each member of this steering team has an equal vote to ensure that no one point of view is given undue weight or influence. Similarly, at Northwest Spring, a small, employee-owned business in Portland, Oregon, the so-called management team is actually composed of managers and employee representatives. In response to the sometimes politically charged and frequently changing mandates issued by Congress, the Rogue River National Forest, an agency of the federal government, is creating 12 geographically defined CARE (Coordinated Area Resource Empowerment) teams that will write the business and project plans for their respective portions of the forest.

Establish effective communication channels that reach all employees. In smaller organizations, a hierarchy of star point teams (described in Chapter Four) can provide this coordination and communication. In larger organizations, E-mail, broadcast fax, teleconferences, and other high-tech means can be invaluable. Where these channels are used regularly (like Federal Express's daily, global teleconference FedEX Overnight),[1] updates on such crises can be handled within the normal course of daily events.

CONCLUSION

While there is no foolproof protection from external events, organizations would be wise to anticipate the unpredictable and put some safeguards in place. The best protection, as implied by the suggestions included in this

---

[1]Frederick Smith, "Creating an Empowering Environment for All Employees," *Journal for Quality and Participation*, June 1990, pp. 6–10.

chapter, is to ingrain self-direction and its values so deeply in the fiber of the organization that it will be impermeable to any attack.

RECOMMENDED READING

Block, Peter. *Stewardship: Choosing Service over Self-Interest.* San Francisco: Berrett-Koehler Publishers, 1993.

Ryan, Kathleen, and Daniel Oestreich. *Driving Fear Out of the Workplace: How to Overcome the Invisible Barriers to Quality, Productivity and Innovation.* San Francisco: Jossey Bass, 1991.

IV

BEYOND
SELF-DIRECTION

Chapter Thirteen

Democracy in the Workplace: Can It Work?

T he Industrial Revolution robbed most workers of much of their power. Pulled from the fields where they set their own schedules to the rhythms of nature, workers became cogs in the machine of mass production. Managers, acting like feudal lords, determined how much and when the employees would work, and they apportioned the fruits of their collective harvest, retaining the lion's share.

Each passing decade brought a new struggle for equity—unions, child labor laws, the eight-hour day, equal employment opportunity, comparable worth—each demand tinged with supplication or adolescent anger, an acceptance of the imbalance of power. While we have imposed legal protections for workers on our leaders, for some inexplicable reason we have accepted tyranny in our workplace within our democratic society.

We vote for the president of the United States, but accept that the board of directors will appoint one of their cronies as president of our organization. We disallow taxation without representation, but permit management to determine what is fair compensation. We make major financial decisions in our households, but then must get three managers' signatures to buy a Bic pen. Even self-directed teams, considered a radical innovation by most, typically assume only the limited powers of a supervisor and remain at the whim of executive strategy. With heads bowed, we have accepted this paradox. In a nation based on equality, we accept that at least in our organizations, some are more equal than others.

Inequality is embedded in our language. Managers are still called *bosses* and *superiors*. Employees are referred to as *subordinates*, *sub* meaning "below" and *ordinaire* meaning "order." Employees are a lower order—like a Neanderthal, we suppose.

However, a confluence of economic and social trends will make organizational democracy increasingly attractive to some. In *Liberation Man-*

agement, Tom Peters describes foundation principles for the organization of the future—what is being called the "virtual corporation" or the "network organization." To respond to the chaotic blur of today's marketplace, many organizations are becoming alliances of networked and autonomous minienterprises. Work revolves around projects in which teams form and disband as needed. Hierarchy and status are obliterated as team members say they "report to each other." In these settings, egalitarian and democratic principles become more easily integrated than in large, bureaucratic megacorporations. For those who need to leverage every ounce of their employees' passion and capabilities, we offer practical guidelines for moving beyond self-direction.

We are under no illusions that our clients will embrace these notions of organizational democracy anytime soon. For many, these concepts seem both impractical and absurd. However, people in that camp can still benefit from becoming familiar with more advanced, extreme versions of empowerment, for we all live inside self-imposed mental boxes that define, among other things, our notions of who should do what. If we know that someone else has traveled far beyond our familiar perimeters and survived, we are more likely to probe the edges of our own boundaries. For the skeptics, we share several stories from beyond.

This chapter is about changing the basic relationship between manager and the managed. We believe that throughout this century, organizations have flowed down a river toward greater empowerment, slowly returning to workers their inalienable rights. While some organizations are trapped in eddies, the path is inevitable. Once you have reached self-direction, organizational democracy, in which workers and management fully share the risks, responsibilities, and rewards, is just around the next bend.

In this chapter, we first clarify the essence of democracy, for the concept has become intertwined with other aspects of our society. Then we share several success stories of democratically run organizations. We wrap up with a discussion of tangible first steps you can take toward a more democratic workplace.

THE ESSENCE OF DEMOCRACY

Just as a fish does not contemplate the water in which it swims, most U.S. citizens do not often reflect on the principles underlying our so-called democratic society. When we mention organizational democracy, people quickly think of voting. But democracy is more than voting, and some of our societal practices have deviated from our democratic principles. Before you can understand organizational democracy, we need to clarify what we mean by democracy itself.

Untangling Democracy from Ourselves

We think of the United States as being a democratic society, but it is not purely so. In fact, our founders held deep suspicions about the common people. "Life, liberty, and the pursuit of happiness" were not really intended for all. "All" meant property owners—those of wealth. Slaves, women, and the poor were not included. While those injustices have since largely been corrected, someone still stands between you and decisions. You vote for senators and representatives, not on the issues themselves. You vote not for the president of the United States but for the electoral college, which then casts your vote for the president. Imbued into our legislative process is a deep distrust of the faculties of the common people such as you and me.

Michael Parenti, a distinguished political scientist and author, compares our system to its precursor, that of the Athenians around 500 BC (*demos*, the Greek word for "the people," is the root of our word *democracy*). Citing our vast unelected bureaucracies, Supreme Court judges appointed for life, secret "national security" budgets of which even most of Congress is ignorant, the executive veto of legislative acts, and our disallowing of evidence in our courtrooms, he states,

> For their part, the Athenians might be astonished at our claim to democracy . . . . The Athenians would have called [some of our practices] tyranny . . . . They would have said, How strange! You've got a long struggle ahead of you to achieve what we got in 461 BC.[1]

The framework of our society provides only partial democracy. This distancing of decision-making power also distances us from our personal responsibility. How easy it is for us to condemn our representatives, to throw the scoundrels out of office, to elect another in whom we have faith —faith with a half-life of their first decision or one month, whichever comes first. In our country, we no longer seek solutions; too often, we

---

[1]Michael Parenti, "The Struggle for Democracy" (Alternative Radio address, Berkeley, CA, October 23, 1992).

place blame. Our children's ignorance is the fault of the schools, say parents, who according to research spend less than one-half hour per day talking and reading to their children.[2] Higher taxes are the fault of the bureaucrats, we cry, as we demand more prison space, better education, and wider roads.

Throughout most of America, we have lost our sense of community, of respect for our interdependence and our personal responsibility to contribute to society. Most Americans, in their relentless pursuit of the elusive American dream, wake to a buzzer, guzzle coffee on their commute, work 10-hour days, catch the last 10 minutes of their kids' ballgames, and return home exhausted in time to fix dinner. They have no energy left to participate in self-governance. At today's frantic pace, democracy is even more difficult to achieve.

Our infatuation with competition further clouds democracy. Our two-party system, for example, builds in structural competition. As Alfie Kohn so well documents in *No Contest: The Case Against Competition*, competition does not often result in better performance. Instead, it erodes self-esteem, creates artificial scarcities, develops hostilities among groups, and encourages cheating. Watergate was only an extreme and public manifestation of the corrupting influence of competition, of viewing others as adversaries.

The essence of democracy is not the vote, or a two-party system, or capitalism per se. Democracy is self-governance: of the people, by the people, for the people—*all* people. It abolishes class distinctions, those with power and those without. It views people as equals, and people view one another as interdependent partners. Organizational democracy is this self-governance within an organization: of the employees, by the employees, for the employees.

More Than Stewardship and ESOPs

In his excellent book *Stewardship*, Peter Block argues convincingly for the partnership approach to leading organizations. He defines stewardship, his alternative to traditional leadership, as "the willingness to be accountable for the well-being of the larger organization by operating in service, rather than in control, of those around us. Stated simply, it is

---

[2]"Not Ready for School," *Oregonian*, July 17, 1994, p. B1.

accountability without control or compliance."[3] But even with his important insights, he stops short of organizational democracy. He states, "Partnership is the willingness to give more choice to the people we choose to serve. Not total control, just something more equal."[4] He even states that some (i.e., managers) are more equal than others.

It is possible to take partnership to the next step: to make everyone equals. For it is somewhat patronizing to talk about treating people as partners when in fact, they are not, or to talk about asking employees to take ownership when in fact they are not owners.

In most organizations, we have separated ownership (represented by stockholders) from decision making (management) and productive work (employees). This separation is at the root of many of our organizational problems, for it places the parties in adversarial positions like a three-way boxing match. In one corner are the stockholders, increasingly represented by institutional traders whose performance is evaluated weekly and who have little interest in the productive work of the organization; they just want the stock price to rise, and their focus is typically short term. In the second corner is management, which must keep the stockholders at bay since their short-term focus often runs counter to the long-term health of the organization. Management is also in a struggle with employees, usually the lightweight in the ring. The less management pays employees, the more money it has to invest in the company and pay out in dividends. Unions, where present, come out swinging from yet a fourth corner.

Fuse these roles and the opposing interests evaporate. Share decision-making authority with employees and make employees owners. Suddenly the focus shifts from mediating between conflicting interests to finding equitable ways to share the harvest. We stop expending our energies against one another and align our energies toward satisfying our customers. There will still be differences of opinion, of course, but far less energy will be wasted in fighting and avoiding other stakeholders.

It is important to note that creating an employee-owned company (ESOP) is not sufficient. Many organizations have given employees stock and then not given them power. In fact, most ESOPs are initiated, planned, and implemented by the top, more often for tax reasons than for

---

[3]Peter Block, *Stewardship: Choosing Service over Self-Interest* (San Francisco: Berrett-Koehler Publishers, 1993), p. xx.

[4]Ibid., p. 32.

reasons of fairness. Ownership without power and participation is a waste of compensation dollars. Ownership *with* power is a potent combination. Creating an ESOP is also not required, as several of the examples in this chapter will show. If you can have only one of the two, choose power over ownership, for there are other ways to share the rewards.

SUCCESSFUL EXAMPLES OF ORGANIZATIONAL DEMOCRACY

Self-directed teams share the responsibilities of a traditional supervisor. What changes with organizational democracy is that employees now share some of the responsibility of executives, including making major strategic decisions: whether to build a new plant, whether to acquire a new business, how to respond to a business downturn. In these organizations, management is not an elite class lording over the kingdom. Instead, managers implement the collective will of members of the organization.

Examples of organizational democracy are few and far between (organizations in Wisconsin, Canada, Brazil, and Spain, for example). However, their successes are dramatic and compelling. We will share several stories that provide an array of options. In some cases, for example, employees receive profit sharing but are not owners. In others, employees own a majority of the organization's stock. In yet others, the *only* owners are employees. Each story will provide a glimpse into the future possibilities for your organization.

Power without Ownership

Thanks to being featured by Tom Peters, the Johnsonville Foods story is quite well known. We repeat it here because many of our other examples are outside the United States. We wanted to eliminate any geographic and cultural excuses. Johnsonville's story is also interesting because sharing significant power in a family-owned business is rare.

Ralph Stayer, owner of Johnsonville Foods, realized that his organization was like a herd of buffalo. Apparently buffalo look to their lead buffalo for direction, so much so that it almost caused their extinction. In the Wild West, after buffalo hunters killed the lead buffalo, all of its followers just stood around waiting to be slaughtered. Instead, Stayer wanted his organization to be like a flock of geese. Geese flying in their V formation use 70 percent less energy than geese flying alone. When the lead goose tires, it falls back, and another goose takes the lead.

It took some time for Stayer to realize he was following the model of the buffalo instead of the goose. As he puts it,

> Now the very things that had brought me success—my centralized control, my aggressive behavior, my authoritarian business practices—were creating the environment that made me so unhappy. I had been Johnsonville Sausage, assisted by some hired hands who, to my annoyance, lacked commitment.[5]

Stayer began turning power over to the employees. Employees took responsibility for setting and meeting performance standards, including coaching and, when necessary, terminating co-workers. They established budgets and decided on capital expenditures. The organization implemented a "pay-for-responsibility" system where people who assumed more responsibilities such as budgeting or training earned additional income. It implemented a "company performance share," a profit-sharing system that paid a fixed percentage of pretax profits on a six-month basis. It also eliminated the terms *employee*, *subordinate*, and *manager*, preferring to use terms such as *members* and *coaches*. As we mentioned in Chapter Three, Stayer also involved employees in setting corporate strategy; the members decided almost unanimously to take over production for a competing plant.

The payback for sharing power has been tremendous. Quality and productivity are both up. A secretary came up with a new product idea and is now running a major new division. Stayer has developed a whole new set of skills, writing books and consulting with other organizations.

Semco has taken organizational democracy even further than Johnsonville Foods. Based in São Paulo, Brazil, Semco manufactures a wide variety of products, including commercial pumps, dishwashers, and air conditioners.

Ricardo Semler, who inherited the organization from his father, operates Semco on three values: trust, transparency, and democracy. Trust is demonstrated by extraordinary freedom. Production employees set their own production quotas and their own hours. Many people even determine their own salaries. Ex-employees who have started spinout ventures work

---

[5]Ralph Stayer, "How I Learned to Let My Employees Lead," *Harvard Business Review*, November–December 1990, pp. 66–83.

on site. There is no dress code. Policies are practically nonexistent. Employees who travel are expected to spend what they need.

Transparency is manifested in unlimited access to information. Everyone's salaries and the corporate books are available for anyone to review. Every six months, employees evaluate their managers and the results are posted. Transparency is physical as well. Instead of walled offices, Semco separates work spaces with a forest of plants.

Democracy provides that employees vote on all major decisions. Whether to open or close a plant, how to respond to tough times, and how much profit sharing should be paid are all decided democratically. Democratic, egalitarian values also affect work. There are no secretaries or receptionists, so everyone fetches coffee, greets guests, types letters, and makes photocopies. That way, no one gets stuck in dead-end jobs. Layers have been reduced from 12 to 3, and corporate staff has been reduced by 75 percent. In his book *Maverick*, Semler explains,

> We've taken a company that was moribund and made it thrive, chiefly by refusing to squander our greatest resource, our people. Semco has grown six fold despite withering recessions, staggering inflation and chaotic national economic policy. Productivity has increased nearly sevenfold. Profits have risen fivefold . . . We have a backlog of over 2,000 job applications, hundreds from people who say they would take any job just to be at Semco.[6]

Obviously, organizational democracy has provided Semco with an enormous competitive advantage.

Ownership and Power (ESOPs)

A number of organizations have let their employees purchase the majority of the organizations' stock, giving them the controlling interest. In fact, it is now estimated that 11 percent of the labor force is covered by an employee stock ownership plan.[7] However, this does not always ensure that employees will have a voice. In the case of a leveraged ESOP (employee stock ownership plans in which the money to buy the stock is

---

[6]Ricardo Semler, *Maverick: The Success Story Behind the World's Most Unusual Workplace* (New York: Warner Books, 1993), p. 7.

[7]Commission on the Future of Labor-Management Relations, *Fact Finding Report* (Washington, DC: U.S. Department of Labor and U.S. Department of Commerce, May 1994), p. 43.

borrowed), the stock is held in trust for the employees, so employees do not actually cast their votes.

Unfortunately, many of these ESOPs were motivated by principles other than democratic ideals: avoiding a hostile takeover, garnering tax incentives, and gaining concessions from employees. For example, a steel mill on the West Coast gained significant prestige and competitiveness by implementing an employee buyout during steel's dog days in the 1980s. With its viability at stake, the tax advantages and employee concessions seemed worth the risk. For awhile, one of its biggest problems was high turnover; employees were becoming millionaires on paper and had to quit to get paid for their stocks. Since then, however, employees' share of stock has dropped to around 25 percent and the organization is run traditionally. Attempts to implement self-directed teams in a portion of the plant have failed due to a lack of management commitment.

Some ESOPs are run democratically, however. Lincoln Electric and the Bureau of National Affairs both have operated as ESOPs for many years and include extensive involvement on the part of employees, including a hand in the governance of the organizations. The best news is that the data indicate that the greater the involvement of employees, the better the performance of these organizations.[8]

Labor-Owned Cooperatives

A labor-owned cooperative is an organization whose only owners are employees. Unlike ESOPs, in which stock can be held by outsiders, these cooperatives link ownership and work. All employees, usually after an introductory or probationary period, pay a membership fee. This fee does not gyrate like a stock price but is set at a reasonable rate so as not to limit the applicant pool to wealthy individuals. Major decisions are made based on a one-person, one-vote basis. A portion of profits is usually allocated to each employee's account, which is then paid when the employee leaves the organization. Often executive pay is set by applying a multiplier to the lowest salary paid to an employee, such as three or seven times.

---

[8]Michael Conte and Jan Svejnar, The Performance Effects of Employee Ownership Plans," in Alan Binder (ed.), *Paying for Productivity* (Washington, DC: Brookings Institution, 1990), pp. 143–82.

A famous example is the Mondragon Cooperatives in Spain. The founder of these cooperatives recognized that funding was often the downfall of most cooperatives known at the time. Eventually the co-ops needed to borrow money to expand, since the only other sources of funds were the limited membership fee and the profits of their venture. And once you borrow from outsiders, you become beholden to them. No longer were the employees the only people with a legal interest in the venture.

To resolve this problem, the Mondragon Cooperatives are formed like satellites around their own bank. Like the urban banks in the United States formed to rejuvenate ghettos, the cooperative bank takes the money deposited by the community and invests it in economic development. The bank offers lower interest rates to socially needed ventures, and if a venture gets in trouble, the bank lowers its interest rate and provides consulting assistance. The venture and the bank sign a partnership agreement promising that neither will abandon the other until the business is profitable. This is in stark contrast to our system, which some describe as "if you don't need the money, we'll lend it to you; if you need the money, you're a bad credit risk."

Ventures are formed by a starter group, people who put forth significant capital and have an existing relationship. (These cooperatives are formed through friendships, the relationship being more important than the specific product or service.) One member of the starter group then spends at least two years with the bank under the wing of a "godfather" who helps write the business plan and a community development plan. After two years of up-front planning, the bank's board of directors decides whether the venture will go ahead.

The employees hired invest approximately one-third of their annual income in the cooperative. While they do not have to pay this up front, as it is deducted from their salary, they would owe the total investment to a bankruptcy court if the venture failed. When a business becomes unviable, workers are not laid off but are retrained for another cooperative venture. This is the essence of sharing the risk, responsibility, and rewards. This is the ultimate in organizational democracy.

But does it work? Absolutely. The Mondragon Cooperatives weathered recessions and disruptive political changes to yield the highest productivity per worker in Spain. The cooperatives produce most of the tools and appliances used in the country. And the bank has not made a bad loan in over 28 years. As Kathleen and William Whyte note in *Making Mondragon*,

Besides the employment growth—from 23 workers in one cooperative in 1956 to 19,500 in more than one hundred worker cooperatives and supporting organizations—their record of survival has been phenomenal—of the 103 cooperatives that were created from 1956 to 1986, only 3 have been shut down. Compared to the frequently noted finding that only 20 percent of all firms founded in the United States survive after five years, Mondragon's survival rate of more than 97 percent across three decades commands attention.[9]

PRACTICAL GUIDELINES

For those who dare to apply democratic principles within their organizations, let us suggest some guidelines from those who have traveled this road before:

- The business concept must be viable. Democracy will not make up for the absence of a market.
- Recognize that the right to make a decision is separate from the competency to implement it. Leadership is still a necessity.
- Clarify what decisions should be made at certain levels, and establish a mechanism to move decisions among these levels.
- Educate and train everyone. Everyone must understand the fundamentals of the business you are in. Interpersonal and meeting skills will also become paramount. Provide resources for training and retraining.
- Codify the principles that will guide you, and establish a mechanism to hold everyone accountable for carrying out those principles.
- Devise a system for resolving conflicts and differences.
- Establish an equitable way for distributing profits or rewards that is consistent with the egalitarian nature of democracy.

CONCLUSION

The examples provided in this chapter prove that organizational democracy does in fact work. It is possible to break the dependency between employee and manager and replace it with an adult partnership. We

---

[9]William Foote Whyte and Kathleen King Whyte, *Making Mondragon: The Growth and Dynamics of the Worker Cooperative Complex* (Ithaca, NY: ILR Press, 1988), p. 3.

believe organizational democracy represents a way to overcome the malaise in our organizations. And as employees assume full responsibility for the health of their organizations, perhaps this attitude will extend to our communities and reinvigorate them.

With the destruction of the Berlin Wall and the Cold War, can we not now break down the office walls and petty conflicts in our organizations? The task has never been so urgent or the potential so great.

RECOMMENDED READING

Adams, Frank, and Gary Hansen. *Putting Democracy to Work: A Practical Guide for Starting Worker-Owned Businesses*. Eugene, OR: Hulogos'i Communications, 1987.

Nirenberg, John. *The Living Organization: Transforming Teams into Workplace Communities*. Homewood, IL: Business One Irwin, 1993.

Parenti, Michael. *The Struggle for Democracy*. Alternative Radio address, Berkeley, CA, October 23, 1992. Transcripts available from Alternative Radio (c/o David Barsamian, 2129 Mapleton, Boulder, CO 80304).

Peters, Tom. *Liberation Management: Necessary Disorganization for the Nanosecond Nineties*. New York: Alfred A. Knopf, 1992.

Semler, Ricardo. *Maverick: The Success Story Behind the World's Most Unusual Workplace*. New York: Warner Books, 1993.

Semler, Ricardo. "Why My Former Employees Still Work for Me." *Harvard Business Review* 27 (January–February 1994), pp. 64–74.

Whyte, William Foote, and Kathleen King Whyte. *Making Mondragon: The Growth and Dynamics of the Worker Cooperative Complex*. Ithaca, NY: ILR Press, 1988.

Index